D1219567

# 童衣選粹
## 中國傳統兒童服飾

# CHILDREN OF THE GODS
## Dress and Symbolism in China

市政局
Urban Council

# 童衣選粹
## 中國傳統兒童服飾

# CHILDREN OF THE GODS
## Dress and Symbolism in China

選自一九九〇年香港博物館所收
嘉麗女士珍藏中國兒童服飾

Chinese Children's Dress from the
Collection of Valery M. Garrett,
acquired by the Hong Kong Museum
of History in 1990

香港博物館籌劃
一九九〇年六月九日至十月廿一日

ⓒ香港博物館編製・香港市政局出版
一九九〇年六月初版，一九九四年六月重印

作者(第一章)：司徒嫣然
　　　(第二章)：嘉麗
編輯：丁新豹
中譯(第二章)：鄭敏儀
展覽籌備：司徒嫣然、鄭敏儀
美術指導：馮熾雄
展覽設計：謝鴻慈
平面設計：陳滙源、萬靜儀
攝影：梁啓堂、陳樹堅
印刷：新輝印務有限公司

Organized by the Hong Kong Museum of History
9th June – 21st October 1990

ⓒ Produced by the Hong Kong Museum of History
Published by the Urban Council, Hong Kong
First published June 1990, reprinted June 1994.

**Authors** (Part I): Naomi Yin-yin Szeto
　　　　　　(Part II): Valery M. Garrett
**Editor:** Joseph Sun-pao Ting
**Chinese Translation** (Part II): Carol Mun-yee Cheng
**Exhibition Management:** Naomi Yin-yin Szeto
　　　　　　　　　　　　Carol Mun-yee Cheng
**Art Direction:** Anthony Chi-hung Fung
**Exhibition Design:** Alvin Hung-chi Tse
**Graphic Design:** Chan Wui-yuen
　　　　　　　　　Janice Ching-yee Man
**Photography:** Leung Kai-tong
　　　　　　　Kris Shu-kin Chan
**Printing:** Sunshine Press Ltd.

# 目錄

# CONTENTS

# 序言

衣、食、住、行是日常生活四大要素，其中居於首位的衣服一項，除了可遮體保暖外，還須講求美觀；服裝的式樣、顏色、裝飾手法，均反映着民族文化的特色及意識形態，在傳統農業社會中，對於子孫繁衍至為重視，故對於兒童的健康成長，極為關注，呵護之情，具體地表現於兒童服裝之上。

在醫藥衞生條件不足的農村，孩童的夭折率很高，傳統上，人們相信幼童夭折是邪魔鬼怪肆虐所致，故兒童的服飾往往綴上吉祥圖案，冀能借助神祇之法力，趨吉避凶，使娃娃能百邪不侵、快高長大。這是民間兒童服飾之一大特色。

天真可愛的娃娃，是家中的寶貝，其所穿的衣服，佩帶的飾物往往由親人一針一線縫製，洋溢着無盡的慈愛，而童衣的色彩繽紛、裝飾豐富多樣，尤在成人服飾之上，極有欣賞價值。

隨着西風東漸，傳統的兒童服飾漸告式微，博物館有見及此，早於年前已在新界蒐集民間傳統服飾。是次，更很高興能得到對中國服飾頗有研究的嘉麗女士慷慨借出其珍藏的童衣及飾物公開展出，此等展品，都是她以多年的努力從新界及中國各地搜集而來。

嘉麗女士既借出珍藏以供展出，復惠賜鴻文，使本目錄生色不少，謹此深致謝意；此外，更蒙鍾燕齊先生、楊廣顯先生及謝克先生借出珍藏，其中施天賜博士更為本目錄中中國兒童習俗淺探一文的英譯稿進行校訂工作，博物館名譽顧問許舒博士提供寶貴意見，也謹此一併致謝。本展覽能順利舉辦，實端賴他們的鼎力支持。

丁新豹
香港博物館館長
一九九〇年五月

# Preface

Clothing, feeding, housing and travelling are regarded by the Chinese as the four basic means of life. Among them, clothing should be the most important one as it comes first in the ranging. Clothes not only keep our body warm but provide us a sense of beauty. Moreover, the cultural tradition and ideology of an ethnic group can be traced from the style, colour and decorative signs of their costumes.

The maintenance of lineal continuity and prosperity is regarded as a matter of utmost importance in traditional Chinese rural society. Consequently, parents will extend great care to their children. The subtlety of parental care can often be reflected on children's costumes.

The mortality rate of children was high in traditional rural villages because of poor medical and hygenic conditions. However, people always believed that the death of children were due to the effect of evils. Therefore, children's costumes are always decorated with auspicious designs which symbolised the presence of supernatural power to deter the evils. This is one of the significant characteristics of children's costumes.

As children are usually the most beloved ones within the family, their clothing and other decorative accessories are often handmade by their parents. Enriched with endless parental love, children costumes are usually more decorative and colourful than the adult ones, and are highly worthy of appreciation.

Traditional Chinese children's costumes have gradually disappeared under the impact of western culture. In order to preserve these valuable cultural items, the Museum of History has been for some years collecting these traditional costumes from the New Territories. We are most grateful to Mrs. Garrett who generously loan us her esteemed collection of children's costumes for display in this exhibition. Mrs. Garrett, with her expert knowledge in Chinese costumes, has spent great effort in collecting these costumes from the New Territories and China.

The Museum would like to extend our warmest thanks to Mrs. V. Garrett for her generous loan of exhibits and contributing an article to the catalogue. We are also grateful to Mr. Joel Chung, Mr. Clement Kwong-ho Yeung, Mr. Derick Hak Tse for their loan of exhibits and particularly Dr. Janet Lee Scott who edited the English translation of the article "Folkways of Chinese Children" in this catalogue. A special vote of thanks is due to Dr. James Hayes, our Honorary Adviser for the expertise advice given. Without their support, this exhibition could never be realized.

Joseph S. P. Ting
Curator, Hong Kong Museum of History
May, 1990

# 前言

**時**至今日，香港以至中國內地的兒童大都穿上西式的童衣，除了間中還可見到兒童仍保留了腳繫銀鈴的習慣、或母親仍採用繡滿花紋的背兒帶外，傳統童衣已告式微。然而，在不久以前的歲月裏，做母親的鮮有不利用種種吉祥圖案和護身符去保佑其初生子女，避免邪魔侵擾的。

事實上，在一九七〇年代晚期，香港農民和漁民已迅速放棄了所穿的傳統服裝，明瞭到此一事實，我決定加以研究，並撰寫了一本有關的書籍。與此同時，我盡量從古玩店、街市攤檔、小販搜藏傳統服飾，更多是從村民直接購得。我搜集了相當數目的童衣和飾物，這些都是母親爲兒女親手縫製的，在兒女長大成人後，母親便把這些東西保留下來，作爲吉祥物，留作紀念。

本人之藏品，基本上是從香港及珠江三角洲搜集而來，亦有不少是從中國其他地方搜得，主要是作對比和比較，但顯然這些服飾都未足以代表整個中國。

在此，衷心感謝許舒博士多年來對我的支持，及他對這個展覽的熱忱。此外，香港博物館總館長何清顯先生提供此一寶貴機會，使我能與廣大市民分享我的藏品，博物館的工作人員給予的幫助；還有我的外子不時予以鼓勵，謹此一併致謝。最後，我必須向新界的村民深深致意，他們把其兒女的童衣及飾物交付給我，我是一定會妥爲保存的。

嘉麗
一九九〇年五月

# Foreword

Today, it is rare to see a Chinese child in traditional dress. Although a few vestiges remain – a silver bell worn round the ankle, an embroidered carrier for a baby – children in Hong Kong, and indeed in most parts of China, wear the latest western fashions. Yet not too long ago it would have been unthinkable on the part of the mother to send her precious child out into the world, unadorned with lucky symbols and thus unprotected from evil all around.

Realization, towards the end of the 1970's that traditional Chinese dress worn by the farming and fishing people in Hong Kong was rapidly disappearing, made me resolve to try to make a record. This research led, eventually, to a book on the subject, and along the way I collected as much as I could, from antique shops, from market stalls and hawkers, but especially from the people themselves. Without any deliberate intent, I found myself amassing quite a sizeable collection of children's wear and accessories, for these were the items often made by the mothers and kept, as a memento and good luck charm, until the child was fully grown.

Inevitably my collection is based on items found in and around Hong Kong and the Pearl River Delta, for this area remains an abiding interest. More pieces came from other parts of China, collected as a contrast and a comparison, but it is not intended to be a China-wide representation.

My sincere thanks go to Dr James Hayes for his unfailing support, as ever, and his enthusiasm for this exhibition. Thanks too are due to Mr C.H.Ho, Chief Curator of the Hong Kong Museum of History for making it possible for my collection to have a wider audience, and for the helpful assistance of the staff at the Museum. Another thank you goes to my husband, Richard for his continuing encouragement. Last but not least, I should like to express my gratitude to all the villagers in the New Territories who, their purpose fulfilled, entrusted me with their children's clothing and charms. They are in safe hands.

Valery M. Garrett
May, 1990

# 中國兒童習俗淺探
# FOLKWAYS OF CHINESE CHILDREN

司徒嫣然 Naomi Yin-yin Szeto

# 引言
# Introduction

"兩兒生四象"銅紙鎮，十七世紀
Bronze paper weight in the shape of a group of four boys, made up of only two heads and two sets of legs, 17th century.

童年生活怎樣影響到個人性格的形成、認知世界與及日後各方面發展，一直以來都是心理學家和社會工作學者所鑽研的重要課題。另一方面，成年人社會的模式可説是兒時生活的延續；反過來，成人羣體的觀念及標準亦透過父母的教養、兄弟、親友和鄰居的接觸及大眾傳媒的潛移默化，慢慢而深刻地影響到孩童的成長。這種錯綜複雜的關係，亦素爲社會學家所關注。

近年來漸有更多民俗學者從文化人類學的角度去研究不同民族的兒童文化，本文現嘗試隨着這方面去探討中國兒童的文化及習俗。誠然，單憑藉年畫上的胖娃娃、剪紙上的母與子、母親手縫的小兒衣物、泥玩偶或風箏等鄉土玩具、民間的廿四孝故事、童話裡面的主角人物……實在未足充份認識中國兒童世界的全豹；尚需要參考史籍文獻、傳世文物及進一步作實地考察。此外，民間文化亦因時間之轉移、地域之不同而有所變異。以下所論及的祇是過往漢族兒童的一般生活禮俗，希望能喚起市民的關注及有興趣人士作更深入的研究。另外，因爲篇幅有限，孩童生活的其他部份例如飲食、學習以至音樂等各方面，亦未能盡錄於文內。

The influence of childhood on individual personality development and cognitive ability has long been a major concern of psychologists and social workers. Undoubtedly, models of adult society can be regarded as continuations of children's culture. On the other hand, the norms and value systems held in the minds of adults greatly affect the child's development through the rearing and modelling relationship between parents and children. In addition, the child is affected by communication and relationships with elder siblings, with elderly relatives and with neighbours, as well as the strong influence exerted by the mass media. Sociologists have placed special attention on and devoted their efforts towards studying this complex of mutual relationships.

In recent years, a growing number of ethnologists have focused on cross-cultural studies of the world's children. Continuing such study, this article will attempt to further penetrate various facets of the life of Chinese children, from the ethnological point of view. Certainly, a neither complete nor competent perception of the reality of the traditional world of Chinese children can be obtained by merely

▷
園亭嬰戲圖
徐操
二十世紀中葉
水墨設色紙本立軸
Children playing in the garden
Xu Cao
mid 20th century
Hanging scroll, ink and
colours on paper

looking at the New Year's woodblock prints of fat and lovely infants. Nor is it sufficient to examine the papercuts in the shape of mother and son, the tiger-shaped infant hats with their elaborate embroidery, the folk toys like claymen and kites, or the major roles played in the famous folk tales "the twenty-four stories of filial piety" – no matter how instructive and attractive such images may be in other contexts. In order to obtain a more comprehensive picture, we must take into consideration historical records and artifacts. Last but not least is the significance of field research, during which interviews can be conducted for the purpose of collecting oral history on the subject. The long history and great distances characterizing the Chinese nation also contributed to the formation of regional differences in folklore. This resulted in the study of folk culture becoming more dynamic and interesting. Recognizing the regional and temporal variations that might arise, this paper will focus only upon those facets of Han Chinese children's life which were commonly shared and known by the majority of the population. However, due to limited space in the present monograph, aspects such as food traditions, the learning process and music involved in Chinese children's life are not included in the following text. It is hoped that this exploration will arouse the public's interest and demand for more intensive surveys on the subject.

# 有關兒童的民間風俗
# Folklore and Children

父母對兒子的寄望殷切，從小便教他讀書寫字，清代《吳友如畫寶》。

At an early age, children, particularly sons, were encouraged to learn how to read and write, from *Wu Youru hua bao* (the woodblock prints by Wu Youru), Qing.

我國素有〝禮義之邦〞的美譽，無論是顯貴的士大夫或是平民百姓，對於儀禮之事，都向來重視。尤其在誕生、嫁娶及喪葬等人生幾個重要階段。

在中國的父系社會裡，生子添丁不單代表了新生命的開端，更是整個家庭的隆重大事，甚至附屬的社羣也沾上了喜氣洋洋的氣氛。另一方面，重男輕女的觀念在傳統社會裡根深柢固。根據《禮記》所載：生了男孩的家庭掛木弓於門左，象徵〝天之尊〞；生了女孩的則掛佩巾於門右，表示〝地之尊〞。此外，《詩經‧小雅‧斯干》載：男孩出生則睡床、穿裳，送以美玉，表示尊貴，是爲弄璋之喜。女孩出生則睡地，包以方布做成的衣服( 褓衣)，送以瓦器紡錘，以示卑順，是爲弄瓦之喜。男丁的誕生，意味着後繼有人，得以傳宗接代，將來可肩負起拜祖祭祀的職責；更且，男丁從小便可協助農耕，增加生產力，改善經濟。成年娶妻後更加添家庭成員及勞動力；又或者十年窗下，一朝高中，更可光宗耀祖，光大門楣。相反，女孩長大後，父母要替她準備嫁妝，把她嫁出去。在這種重男輕女觀念的影響之下，一般誕生或成長過程中的禮儀習俗，基本上祇指男童而言。

在貧窮的村落裡，嬰兒的出生夭折率及患病死亡率非常高，父母對小兒的期望殷切，因此孩童誕

China has long been given the name "The Country of Etiquette and Righteousness", wherein ceremonies and rites were strictly observed by all strata of the society, from the elite to the general populace. The rites commemorating the most significant transitions of human life - birth, marriage and death – were particularly elaborate.

In traditional Chinese patrilineal society, the birth of a son not only symbolized the beginning of a new life, but was treated as more than a family affair in that it would bring happiness to the entire community. The preference for sons was a sentiment deeply rooted in the traditional thinking of the Chinese. According to *The Book of Rites*, a wooden bow would be hung to the left of the family's doorway when a son was born, symbolizing that the birth was as honourable as the heavens. A kerchief was hung to the right of the doorway for a girl, signifying that the birth was only as honourable as the earth. Moreover, a poem of *The Book of Songs* recorded that in ancient China, the newly-born son had the right to sleep on the bed, to wear decent clothing and to be given a piece of fine jade as an emblem of honour. The parents were also congratulated on the happiness of "having

生、成長及保育的習俗的另一功能，是寄予父母們心靈上的安定和保障。簡而言之，圍繞生子之俗，一是〝賀〞：祝賀及慶祝小兒的誕生。二是〝忌〞：遵行禁忌，避免一切可妨礙孩子成長的行爲。三是〝壽〞：求諸神明靈界或在日常生活中，小心翼翼，祝福孩子他日長命百歲。

a piece of fine jade" (i.e., having a son born). On the other hand, a newly-born girl was left to sleep on the ground, was wrapped in rough swaddling clothes and given a curved tile, used as a spindle weight, to show her inferiority. The parents were greeted as having the happiness of "having a piece of tile" (i.e., having a daughter born).

From the traditional Chinese point of view, a son would, in the future, sire more sons to continue the family line and bear the responsibilities of worshipping the ancestors. Moreover, a son would improve the household economy by providing additional manpower through his own and his wife's labour. If a son studied hard, he might even become an official, attaining the highest position in the Confucian hierarchy, and acquiring prestige and glory for the entire family, clan and ancestors. On the other hand, female children were most looked upon as burdens on whom the family must spend money to feed and to raise and who in the end would marry into someone else's home with a dowry supplied by the parents. As a result of the traditional Chinese preference for male offspring, most of the rituals and customs practised at birth and during the development of the child were directed to male children only.

△

年幼的兒子往往備受家人的寵愛及特別的照顧。在清代關庭昌所繪的水粉畫中可看到當時的一位婢女用傳統的背兒帶背着少主人，及從女主人手中接過〝撥浪鼓〞（〝撥浪鼓〞是早期民間玩具之一）。

古代用來背負小兒的東西泛稱〝襁褓〞，〝襁〞指布幅而〝褓〞即爲被子。早在秦時，〝襁褓〞已廣爲婦女所用，近代卻多流行於華南地區。

△

Infant sons, considered as vulnerable members and treasures of the family, were given special attention. This gouache by Tingqua of the 19th century depicts a maid carrying an infant on her back with a traditional baby carrier and receiving from her mistress a *bolanggu*, one of the earliest kind of toys in China.

In ancient times, the device for carrying a baby on one's back was generally called *qiangbao* where *qiang* and *bao* literally meant a "strip of cloth" and "quilt" respectively. *Qiangbao* were widely used by women as early as the Qin Dynasty and became more popular in South China in the last century.

In destitute rural villages where the occurrence of premature child death was great, the aspirations of parents towards their children were particularly keen. The customs relating to birth and growth as well as those practised to ensure a healthy infant served to offer the parents at least some psychological assurance. The three major components incorporated in the series of

15

## 嬰兒誕生及成長過程中的禮俗

### 誕生禮

嬰兒出生後數天,均不出產房(通常是母親房內),只有至親前來祝福和探望,而新生兒將來的性格,會與第一個進門探訪的外人或親戚相近,稱之為〝踩生〞。

### 接三朝及洗三

嬰兒出生三日稱為〝三朝〞,外婆家送紅喜蛋祝賀。當日又有〝洗三〞儀式。北方人以艾葉、花椒等草藥湯洗嬰兒,邊洗邊唸祝辭,以驅災避邪。

### 滿月及剃頭禮

在孩子滿月之日,外婆家會送來新的衣、帽、鞋,還有被褥等賀禮。當天並舉行剃頭禮,嬰兒剃頭的風俗,早在宋代已流行。剃頭時,請一位有福氣的親友(通常是兒孫滿堂的)抱著小孩,坐在廳堂中央,由剃頭師將胎髮慢慢剃下,而剃下的胎髮則盛於小袋中,並用紅綠花線穿起來,掛於堂屋高處或床前。新生兒隨即換上色彩鮮艷的新衣,父母設宴款待親友,分發紅喜蛋,而親友亦以具有吉祥兆頭的禮品到賀。

▽
長命鎖
Padlocks symbolizing longevity

birth rites were: "celebration", "taboo" and "longevity". "Celebration" usually referred to the rituals and ceremonies celebrating the birth of a child, whilst "taboo" was interpreted as the prohibitions on both parent and child from doing anything that might do harm to or cause difficulties in the raising of the child. The desire for "longevity" was secured through an appeal to the ancestors or the supernaturals, or through daily practices designed to secure good fortune and long life for the child.

## The Rites Directed to Childbirth and Child Development
### The ritual of birth

During the first few days, the newly-born baby usually remained in the mother's room, and only a limited number of intimate relatives were allowed to visit and express good wishes to the mother and child. It was also believed that the personality of the infant would be modelled on that of the first visitor, a custom known as *caisheng*.

### The ritual of the third day

On the third day after the birth, red-dyed eggs were sent by the maternal grandmother to the new born's family as a gift celebrating the birth. The custom of *xisan* (washing the baby on the third day of birth) was popular in North China. In this ritual, the adults washed the baby with a soup of mugwort and Chinese prickly ash, with the intent of simultaneously exorcizing demons and blessing the baby with good fortune.

### The full moon and the ritual of shaving the head

When the baby was one month old, gifts in the

## 百晬

嬰兒誕生至一百日時，外婆及親友都會送上長命鎖、長命衣等禮物祝賀。家人亦開筵作慶，分發紅喜蛋。嬰兒被稱為〝百歲兒〞，以祝福小兒他日長命百歲。

## 周晬及抓周禮

小兒滿一歲的儀式稱為〝周晬〞。當日親友齊集，小兒穿上新衣，舉行〝抓周〞禮。首先由小孩父母焚香拜祭祖先，於桌或地上陳列各種物件，其中包括玩物和生活用品等，任由小兒抓取，由此推測其日後的興趣、志向和前途。若小孩抓著文房四寶，人們便相信他將來會知書識墨，博取功名。

▽
抓周禮
The *zhuazhou* ceremony

form of new clothes, hats, shoes and blankets would be sent by the maternal grandmother. The ritual of shaving the infant's head, which was popular as early in the Song Dynasty, was carried out on the day of the full moon. The infant was held by a blessed relative or friend (usually an elderly person having many sons and grandchildren) who sat in the middle of the main hall. The barber then cut the child's hair. The hair trimmings would be put in a tiny bag sewn with red and green threads and then hung high above the hall or at the side of the bed. The child was then dressed in colourful new clothes. In addition to the red-dyed eggs, the relatives and friends invited to the ceremony were given a feast at the end of the day. Gifts with auspicious meanings were also presented by the relatives and friends to the parents of the child.

### The ritual of a hundred days

When the infant reached the age of one hundred days, gifts such as padlocks and new clothes symbolizing long life would be given by the maternal grandmother, the relatives and friends. A feast was then provided by the family to entertain the guests and red-dyed eggs were again distributed during the ceremonies. The child was called "a child of one hundred years" symbolizing longevity.

### The first birthday and *zhuazhou* ceremony

At the age of one year, the child was made to carry out the *zhuazhou* ceremony in the presence of relatives and friends. One of the parents held the beautifully-dressed baby in his/her arms and made him bow before the ancestral shrine. Then the baby was set in the centre of a huge round table or on the ground

在八〇年代香港新界的一些村落里，仍保留了"點燈"的習俗。

The custom of "hanging up the lantern" is still practised in certain New Territories villages in Hong Kong

四位穿上傳統服裝及戴上耳環的香港蜑家小女孩

Four little girls of the boat people of Hong Kong, in traditional clothing and wearing earrings.

### 開燈

在華南地方，特別是廣東一帶，在去年生了男孩的人家，於元宵節時會具備牲酒，把燈掛在宗祠或廟堂，祀神祭祖。燈與"丁"語音相近，"點燈"的意義是要把新添的男丁正式加入族系裡，並設宴與親友歡敍，稱爲"燈酒"。

### 及笄

笄是古代婦女盤頭用的簪子。古代女子到了十五歲時，把頭髮簪起，表示已成年。近代已沒有流行這禮儀。

### 冠禮

古代男子到二十歲時，即由父親或長輩主持加冠的禮節，象徵着已進入成年，社會亦予以承認、管理和約束，並可擇偶婚配和有權利參加祭祀。這禮儀在近代已趨式微，只有一些少數民族中仍保留著與漢族冠禮相似的禮儀。

## 禁忌與保育

民間有關保護兒童的禁忌與習俗實在不勝枚舉，以下列舉較常見的幾項：

### 與衣、食有關的風俗

民間的孩子除了戴虎頭帽、穿獸頭鞋之類以驅邪外，母親還替小孩戴上金或銀的耳環，銀、銅或鐵製的腳鐲及頸項圈。因爲耳環與腳鐲等被認爲是神的刑具，可用來鎖著小兒的魂魄，以保長壽。有時腳鐲上還附有銀鑾鈴，使小兒走動時發出鈴聲，以嚇走邪魔。（在華南地區，特別是在海上生活的漁民，母親可憑着孩兒腳上的銀鈴所發出的聲響，辨別小兒活動位置的遠近，以防止兒童不慎墮海。）父母又把鑄有"長命百歲"字樣的"長命鎖"掛於孩子頸上，將小兒"鎖住"，避免其被邪神惡魔帶走。

surrounded by an assortment of articles such as toys, stationery, herbs, and so on. The child was encouraged to pick up anything he liked and whatever article he grasped was considered as an indication of his character in later life, and of the various professions he might enter. For example, if a brush was chosen, the child might become a scholar when he grew up.

### The hanging of lanterns

In South China, particularly Guangdong Province and nearby areas, the family who had had a son born during the previous year would prepare a sacrifice of a domestic animal such as a chicken for worshipping the ancestors during the Lantern Festival (the fifteenth day of the Lunar New Year). A special lantern was hung in the ancestral hall or village temple to announce the birth of the new-born of the previous year. As the word "lantern" is a homonym for *ding* which means "son", the hanging of the lantern in the ancestral hall formally introduced the son to the ancestors and the clan and allowed the child to be included and recorded in the family line. A feast called "the banquet of lanterns" was also held, in which the entire community enjoyed itself.

### The ritual of putting on *ji*

*Ji* was the name for women's hairpins in ancient times. In the early days, girls at the age of fifteen had to fix up their hair using these hairpins, namely, *ji*. So doing symbolized the beginning of adulthood. This ancient rite of initiation had faded in recent dynasties.

### The ritual of putting on the hat

During this special initiation rite, the father or an elderly relative from the family would place

其他與衣食有關的是〝討百家飯〞、〝穿百家衣〞和〝戴百家鎖〞的習俗。在舊社會裡,爲了使孩子容易養育,父母多向鄉裡各家討取米糧煮成百家飯給孩子吃;零布縫成百家衣給孩子穿;以及將銅錢用五色綫編成鎖形;又或將收集起來的錢購一銀鎖掛於嬰兒頸項。依民間信仰,孩子年少體弱,得吃百家飯、穿百家衣和戴百家鎖,俾能集眾家之力,抗邪避害。

兒童頭戴虎頭帽、腳踏獸鞋及玩布虎爲樂,藉此驅走邪魔,清代《吳友如畫寶》。

Children wearing a tiger hat, animal shoes and playing with a rag stuffed toy tiger for warding off evil spirits, from *Wu Youru hua bao*, Qing.

a hat on the head of the boy at the age of twenty, marking his entry into adulthood. The young man was then allowed to assume the privileges of adulthood, including marriage and participation in ancestral worship. On the other hand, the young man was expected to behave according to the social norms and standards of the society. Nowadays, this ceremony is seldom held among the Han Chinese, and reference must be made to certain minority nationalities for similiar initiation rites.

## Taboos and Child-rearing Customs

There was a multitude of taboos and child-rearing customs invoked for the protection of children in traditional Chinese society. Some common examples are given below:

### Customs concerning clothing and food

In addition to wearing tiger hats and animal shoes as a protection against evil, the child would also wear ornaments: gold or silver earrings, and silver, brass or iron anklets and necklaces especially chosen by the mother. The earrings and anklets were considered as implements for the punishment of the gods and as such were able to lock the child to the earth. The longevity of the son could therefore be ensured. Sometimes anklets were made with bells, so that the sound produced by the bells when the child moved about could frighten off the evil spirits. For the boat people of South China, the sound produced by the bells on the anklets had another function, in that it could assist the mother working on board to keep track of her son, ensuring that he would not fall into the sea. It was also the custom for a Chinese child to wear around his neck a padlock inscribed with the characters "to live as long as

19

清末及本世紀初流行於中國各地的不同形狀及刻有吉祥
文字及圖案的壓勝錢

Coins, given to the children on the eve of the New
Year. From different regions of China, they are in
various shapes and inscribed with auspicious
patterns and characters, late Qing and early 20th
century.

▷

"五毒"墊繡小兒背心（背面），西安，陝西省。

A child's waistcoat appliquéd with the "five
poisons" (the back side), Xian, Shaanxi Province.

## 時節習俗

長輩們每於除夕夜把紅紙包著的壓歲錢送給兒
童，或在小孩睡着後，把錢壓在枕頭下面，藉以賄
賂可能出現的魑魅魍魎。相傳此舉能驅邪求祥，避
免兒童被年獸所傷害。

傳統民間習俗以農曆五月爲惡月，因爲此月份多
雨潮濕，瘟疫滋蔓，邪魔逞凶。每逢端午時份，五毒
（蝎子、蜥蜴、蜈蚣、蛇及蟾蜍）便會出動害人，小孩
最易成爲五毒傷害的對象。習俗上使小孩們逃避
五毒侵害的方法有：（一）貼"五毒"剪紙或繫五色
綫於小孩臂上；（二）父母替小孩穿上繡有五毒圖
樣的衣服，實行以毒攻毒；（三）小孩佩帶彩袋香
包，袋裡裝著雄黃、香藥等，以禳祛邪魔，降服鬼怪
和防疫避毒。

a hundred years", ensuring longevity. In early Chinese society, the parents tried every means to ensure the survival of their children. Some of these methods were known as asking for "Hundred Families Rice", wearing "Hundred Families Coat" and "Hundred Families Padlock". For the first, bits of rice were gathered from different families and cooked as food for the child; in the second, strips of cloth were given from these families and sewn into the child's clothes; for the latter, cash coins were gathered, to be either arranged in the shape of a padlock using five-coloured threads, or used to buy a silver padlock which was hung around the child's neck. It was a folk belief that with the efforts of a hundred families, the vulnerable child might become strong and powerful, able to keep away the demons.

### Festival customs

On the eve of the Lunar New Year, a coin wrapped in a piece of red paper was given to the child by the parents or other elderly members of the family. Sometimes, the coin was placed as a surprise underneath the child's pillow after he had fallen asleep. The purpose was to bribe the evil spirits and the "beast of the New Year" to ensure that they would not hurt the child throughout the year.

The fifth month of the Lunar Calendar was, in the Chinese folk tradition, a month of wickedness during which the weather was humid, when plagues and pestilences proliferated and evil spirits became more abundant. As the fifth day of the fifth month (the Dragon Boat Festival) approached, the "five poisons" representing the scorpion, lizard, centipede, snake and toad (or spider; the specific insects vary from region to region) were active and threatened to harm the children. People would therefore use the images of these noxious creatures to frighten away these same five poisonous beings. It was also customary to perform the following actions for the children in order to ensure their safety. First, papercuts of "five poisons" or five-coloured threads were attached to or fastened around the children's arms. Second, aprons, collars, hats and other items of clothing were embroidered with images of the "five poisons" and worn. Finally, tiny fragrant bags embellished with embroidery and containing herbs were carried by the children.

**Naming of the child**

Although the baby was usually named shortly after birth, it was not until the age of initiation (twenty for boys and fifteen for girls) that a second, proper, name was given. Some parents wished to have their children named after immortals or gods, to ensure their protection against diseases, misfortune and mortality. An infant name (or "milk name") was also commonly given by traditional Chinese families. Names with other auspicious implications were most welcome by the parents, such as "the son of nobility" and "the son of the dragon" in the northern region. Humble or even derogatory names like "puppy" were also employed by parents as a means of fooling the evil spirits into thinking that the child was only an animal, not a human, and therefore not worth harming. Names with the meaning of charms like "lock the child to the pillar" or "root of the earth" would have the neutralizing effect of using evil against evil. In the southern provinces, the baby and an auspicious object were put together on the scale, and the total weight (such as "six

## 命名

嬰兒誕生後,便須命名。待男子到二十歲行冠禮及女子到十五歲行笄禮時,再取字。

有些父母用神佛的名稱給誕生的小孩命名,象徵把孩子交予神靈保護,使他避開災難、疾病及夭折。命名之外,又有取乳名的習俗。一般父母均是取吉祥的名字:在北方的,如〝貴兒〞、〝龍仔〞等。有些父母則選擇一些〝賤〞名,如〝小狗〞之類,希望取了賤名的孩子不易被瘟神病魔看中而奪走。此外,若爲孩子取了符咒意義的名字,如〝鎖柱〞及〝土根〞等,則有相生相尅之效,以求平安成長。有些南方人,把嬰兒與吉祥物放在一起,用秤量過,以所得斤兩爲乳名－例如〝六斤〞、〝九斤〞等－習俗上稱爲〝上籃秤〞。

▽
秤小孩重量,清代《吳友如畫寶》。
江南人士除了喜歡把小兒的重量作爲其乳名外,南方的水上人家更愛把小孩的出生日期改成名字,例如"初三"等。

The weighing of a child, from *Wu Youru hua bao*, Qing.
The weight of an infant was sometimes used as his infant name ("milk name").
In addition, the boat people of South China often named their baby according to the date of the birth such as, "the third day of the month".

▽
小孩由年長婦女陪伴下往神廟進香求福，清代《吳友如畫寶》。
各地的保育神祇包括有牀公牀母、送子觀音和金花娘娘……等。

A child in full costume, accompanied by elderly women, on their way to the temple to wish for good fortune, from *Wu Youru hua bao*, Qing. The deities devoted to the protection of childbirth and the growth of children included the God and Goddess of the Bed, Goddess of Mercy and the Golden Flower Empress... etc.

## 香火、仙丹及其他

遇上小兒患病，習俗上又有把在神廟香爐燒剩下來的香腳，縫成一小包袱狀，串上紅繩，掛在小兒身上。又有用香灰以茶和之，給小兒吃，以求孩兒痊癒。

多病的孩兒，父母把他的生時日月，交給算命先生收禁，或替小孩認一些多子女人家的父母爲乾爹乾娘，以祈孩童容易養活，並長命百歲。

## Joss sticks and candles, elixir of life and others

Parents in traditional Chinese society might turn to the supernatural when their children were sick. A tiny bag containing pieces of the stems left over from the burning of the incense sticks in the temple would be hung around the neck of the child with a red thread. The alternative way to cure the sickness was to feed the child with a mixture of incense ashes and water. In the case of a child who was always falling ill, the parents would disclose his date of birth to a fortune-teller in the temple, hoping that he would take care of the health of the child in the future. Moreover, men and women with abundant offspring were invited to be the godparents of the child, for the purpose of wishing the child long life.

# 兒童髮式
# Children's Hairstyles

從歷代的人物及風俗畫、百子及嬰戲圖,甚至近代的民間年畫中,都可發現一系列趣緻可愛,千奇百怪的兒童髮式。根據沈從文教授《中國古代服飾研究》書中載:古代小孩和未成年男女,頭髮多作小丫角,或稱〝總角〞、〝丱角〞。安陽文化館有一相傳爲商代的雕玉小孩,頭作雙丫角,估計是目前所見最早的一種式樣。又據《禮記》中載:「三月之末,擇日剪髮爲鬌:男角、女羈;否則男左、女右」。即小兒的胎髮在一定期限內必須剪去,但留下其中一部份,稱爲〝鬌〞。鬌的形狀與位置,視男女而異,其中一式是男孩留兩簇髮,各在腦門(俗稱〝囟門〞,即頭正中與前額之間)一旁,或結成小丫角,稱爲〝角〞;女孩則在頭頂正中留一小撮髮,縱橫相交,編成小辮,名爲〝羈〞。另一款式是男女皆留下一簇髮,男的在左,女的在右。

由此可見,在宋代甚至較早,我國已有小兒剃頭而留下小部份頭髮的習慣。同時,我們從清代的宮廷畫與及天津楊柳青年畫之娃娃集,更可觀察到當時的社會,上達皇侯子孫,下至平民百姓子女,小兒剃頭的現象甚爲普遍。過往民間小兒的基本剃頭式樣,其中包括以下幾項:

The centuries-old Chinese portraits and paintings of "a hundred sons" and "infants playing", and the New Year pictures of recent years have allowed a record to be kept of the multitude of amusing and peculiar hairstyles of children. According to Professor Shen Cong-wen's book on ancient Chinese costume, during historical periods the *xiaoyajiao* was the most popular hairstyle for both small children and youngsters. *Xiao* literally means "small", *ya* means "bifurcation", *jiao* means "horn", so as a whole *xiaoyajiao* was a pair of bifurcated horns. A child's figure in jade in the Cultural Institute of Anyang depicts this particular kind of hairstyle, supposedly the earliest style seen for Chinese children. *The Book of Rites* also recorded that the hair of a newly-born baby had to be removed within a certain period of time, leaving a portion of the hair called *duo*. The shape and location of the *duo* were determined by the sex of the baby. One kind, for boys, was to have two bunches of hair remaining unshaved, one above each ear. These tufts of hair could also be put up as a pair of *xiaoyajiao*; the tufts of hair were made into a pair of small bifurcated horns. Girls would have one bunch of hair right in the centre (central part) of the skull, criss-crossed to form a plait

△
從河南省博物館所藏的宋代白釉彩繪童子，可見當時流行的其中一款兒童髮式。

Children's hairstyle in vogue in the Song Dynasty as shown in this porcelain child figure with pigments in white glaze made in the Song Dynasty, now in the collection of the Henan Provincial Museum.

（1）在腦門（頭頂與前額之間的部份）留下一簇（撮）頭髮，其餘剃光，多見於男孩。

（2）在腦門的左、右或兩旁均留下一簇頭髮，其餘剃光。

（3）在頂心（頭頂）留下一簇頭髮，其餘剃光。

（4）在後腦留下一簇頭髮，其餘剃光。

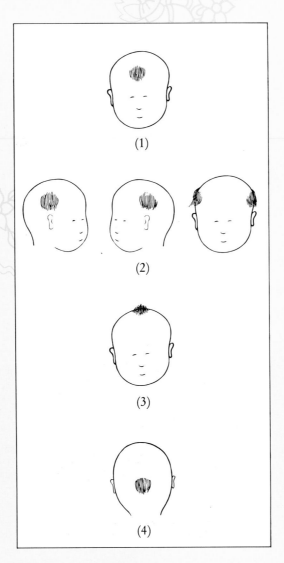

(1)

(2)

(3)

(4)

called a *ji* (a bridle). Variations in style also occurred such as the boy's style with a tuft on the left of the skull above his ear while the girl's style would have a bunch of hair over her right ear.

The custom requiring infants to have their hair shaved, with only tufts of hair remaining, had been practised as early as the Song Dynasty or possibly even earlier. Both paintings of royalty and the series of infants depicted in the New Year Pictures of Yangliuqing in Tianjin provided evidence of the prevalence of the traditional hairstyles of Qing society. Both royal descendants and the children of the general populace shared similar hairstyles.

The basic hairstyles for infants in the past, from which variations were derived, are illustrated as follows:

(1) To have the head bald with a bunch of hair remaining unshaved at the *naomen* (literally "the doorway to the brain", the position between the top of the skull and forehead). This hairstyle was commonly seen among male infants.

(2) To have the head bald with one or two bunches of hair remaining unshaved on either the left, right, or both sides of the skull above the ears.

(3) To have the head bald with a bunch of hair remaining unshaved on the top of the skull.

(4) To have the head bald with a bunch of hair remaining unshaved at the rear of the skull.

隨著以上的基本式樣,幼兒髮式可再演變成爲更複雜的類別(可參考宋蘇漢臣之嬰戲圖系列及近代年畫等),例如:當剃剩的頭髮長了,散著的會披散飄揚,不大方便,便結成小髻並用有色絲繩繫着、編成小辮子,或結成小丫角。

Certainly, variations in style could be derived from the above basic elements, to provide more variety. For example, when the tuft(s) of hair grew, the long hair might cause inconvenience. To prevent this, the bunch(es) of hair could be worn into small buns fastened and decorated with coloured threads, braided or put up as *xiaoyajiao*.

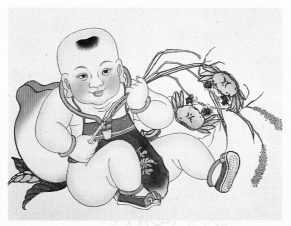

△
清代的小兒髮式可在天津楊柳靑年畫之娃娃集中略見一斑

△
Various infants' hairstyles of the Qing Dynasty were depicted in the "Series of Infants" set of the Yangliuqing New Year pictures of Tianjin.

Both the custom of shaving the heads of infants and children, and the resulting uniqueness of the hairstyles, may be better understood if certain background beliefs are kept in mind.

## (1) Beliefs and Customs

In traditional Chinese society, the process of giving birth to a child was believed to be impure. The hair of the newly born was, therefore, also regarded as dirty and had to be shaved or otherwise removed. The hair trimmings would be kept in a secret place (in the same manner as the afterbirth and umbilical cord) so that the hair would not be taken away by evil spirits or wild animals which might bring bad luck to the infant. According to folk belief, evil demons could cause harm to the infant by working on his hair. Wild animals such as owls were active during the night when the moonlight was dim and the wind was strong. Unlucky children would be caught and taken away as the evil spirits or the owls grasped their hair. For protective purposes, the hair of the infants was usually shaved or made into a pair of *xiaoyajiao* (small bifurcated horns). The evil spirits were fooled into thinking that the infant was only an animal with two horns on its head, and thus not worth harming. Some parents believed that they could prevent their children from being caught away by grasping the little braids; others believed that the braids worn by the child were too tiny and short to be seized by the demons and wild animals.

In his book, *Exorcising the Trouble Makers: Magic, Science and Culture,* Professor Francis L.K. Hsu points out that traditional Chinese culture inclined towards religion, in that even

至於歷代小兒因剃髮而漸形成獨特髮式的背境成因及功能,可從以下不同角度來探討:

## (一)信仰及習俗

在傳統社會裡,生產被視作不潔,古人並且相信胎髮是污穢的,所以有除去的必要。他們認爲胎髮能影響到小兒自身,故剪下來的胎髮如胞衣或臍帶之類,都須慎重收藏起來,免遭外人或邪魔鳥獸侵害。又據民間傳說,妖魔鬼怪之輩會奪取小孩頭髮,加以傷害。例如貓頭鷹會在月黑風高的晚上,抓著童髮,藉以搶走或襲擊小孩,爲了保護孩童性命，遂把頭髮剃去。又或者梳成小丫角，使小孩看來只像頭上有角的野獸，把四周那些要難爲小兒的鬼怪們騙倒。還有一些傳說是父母可抓著孩兒的小辮，把他從邪魔處奪回來，甚至因爲小兒的辮子短小，忽忽走過的魯莽鬼怪亦難於捉住。

然而人類學家許烺光教授在其 *Exorcising the Trouble Makers: Magic, Science and Culture* 一書中曾指出，在中國社會裡，有很多從科學實證所得的知識是用了宗教的意念( 從現今的角度來看是迷信 )去包裝。中國兒童剃頭的種種風俗，其實亦有其科學因素存在。

## ( 二 )保護作用

小兒留髮的部位通常在頭的前、頂、兩旁及後腦部份，這正是小孩頭上最重要的位置。例如頭的兩側，孩童玩要時易受磨擦、撞碰，或不慎跌在地上，撞傷後腦。尤其是在所謂〝腦門〞的地方，嬰兒初生時，頭顱骨尚未牢固縫合，在〝腦門〞處仍可見到神經跳動的情形。這些幼嫩而又易受損傷的頭部位置，最直接的保護方法就是利用天然的頭髮遮蓋。

▽
山東省高密縣農村婦女手造的剪紙，顯示出當地的孩童髮式。

Papercuts made by local peasant women from Gaomi County, Shandong Province, showing children's hairstyles of the region.

empirical knowledge was always interpreted as a form of religious belief. In the case of children's hairstyles, although they were justified in terms of traditional customs and creeds, they also reflected certain aspects of Chinese people's empirical (or scientific) knowledge related to children's health.

## (2) The Protective Function of Hair

The positions where bunches of hair usually remained unshaved were in the front, at the top, on the two sides and at the rear of the child's skull, positions which were considered as the most important parts of the head. The two sides of the head would be easily hurt if children bumped into each other at play while the rear of the skull would also be injured in the case of falling to the ground. Particularly for the new-born babies, the position between the top of the skull and the forehead (so-called "doorway to the brain") was most vulnerable to injury, as this part of the skull had not yet merged and the beatings of the nerves could be felt. Undoubtedly to protect these areas, it was most direct and effective to use the natural hair.

## (3) Physical Development

The frequent shaving of hair during the infant stage helped to stimulate the growth of hair and the hair would eventually become dense and dark. Traditionally, a person with exuberant, dense and dark hair was believed to have a sturdy body.

△
兒童以捉頭蝨為樂，十九世紀末。

Children catching each other's headlice for fun,
late 19th century.

▷
清末在北方常見之其中十二款兒童髮式
隨着年紀的增長，孩童不再易受邪魔藉着頭髮侵害，因
而開始留髮，在民間逐流傳了層出不窮的髮式。

Twelve popular children's hairstyles of the northern
regions of China during the late Qing period.
As children became older, evil spirits could no
longer easily harm the child through his hair.
Children's hair could then be grown longer and
made up into a variety of hairstyles.

## （三）生理成長

孩童時期常剃髮，能刺激到將來頭髮生長旺盛，成
年時，頭髮會變得濃密而烏黑。傳統上，中國人相
信濃而黑的頭髮標誌著強健的體魄。

## （四）個人衛生

古代居住環境簡陋，衛生設施不足，小孩剃頭之舉
實有助於杜絕頭蝨的滋生及蔓延，留下的一或數
撮頭髮，打理比較方便。

基於以上各種原因，小孩剃頭的儀式，經歷了千百
年，流傳下來，成為傳統的一部份。最後更發展為
清末多姿多采的兒童髮式，百花齊放。

## (4) Personal Hygiene

The ancient Chinese were sheltered in quarters
with insufficient sanitary facilities. The custom
of shaving the child's hair made it easier to
control the spread of headlice. The bunches of
hair left could be treated with ease should
infection occur.

Consequently, it was due to the factors and
functional purposes mentioned above that the
"shaving" custom for children survived over the
centuries in China, eventually developing into
the various lovely hairstyles of Chinese children
seen in the Qing Dynasty.

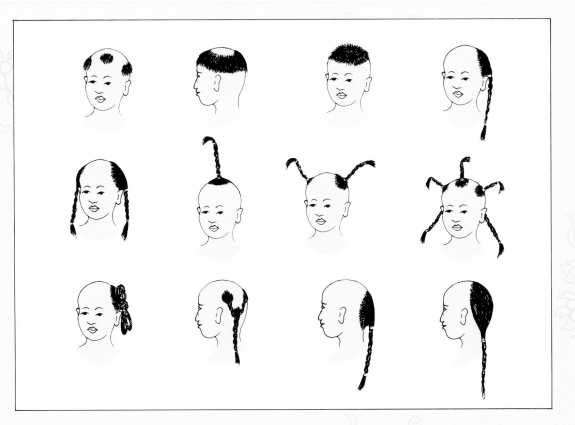

# 象徵與傳說
# Symbols and Legends

母與子的密切關係,普遍反映於世界各文化之中。在傳統中國社會裡,母親對下一代的殷切寄望,單從她們替孩兒縫造的各種衣飾及日用品,可見一斑。雖然精緻的刺繡手工,可表現婦女賢德端雅的一面,但是更具意義的是農村婦女透過她們費盡心思替小兒設計縫造的衣飾物品,充份反映出母親對孩兒的無比關懷。尤其是兒子在家庭裡佔着重要地位,並得到母親的特別呵護。我們不難在環繞着小兒生活的衣服、玩具等發現到一些常用的圖案或形象,其中附著深遠而豐富的象徵意義。例如在衣飾取材方面,龍

▷
母親在大除夕替小兒趕縫"士人"帽,
清代《吳友如畫寶》。

Mother sewing a scholar hat for her child on the eve of the New Year, from *Wu Youru hua bao*, Qing.

The intimate bonding between mother and child seems to be true for every culture of the world. In particular, mothers in traditional Chinese society placed great hopes on their children. Part of the expectations of the mother for her children could be best reflected in the embellishing of the clothing and daily necessities she made for them. Apart from the fact that, in traditional China, remarkable embroidery skills and abilities of women were thought to reflect their finer qualities and inner natures, it is also important to appreciate the loving care shown by the peasant woman towards her children through these items of clothing and headgear. Owing to the important role male descendants played in traditional families, sons received special attention and greatest care from the mother. Therefore, it was not surprising to find a series of patterns and images frequently used by these "folk artists", depicting the desires and hopes of mothers towards the future of their sons. Of these images the dragon had been so closely associated with the emperor that it rarely appeared in folk art. However, the phoenix and mandarin duck were frequently used as the motifs for baby carriers depicting hopes for long-lasting marriage and fertility. Some

29

△
母親會替小兒縫造一些內藏蕎麥殼的枕頭，作用是令睡枕乾爽，並可矯正幼兒的頭型。
圖右：河北省石家莊的雙頭虎枕，可保護酣睡的小兒免受邪魔的騷擾。若小孩遇有惡夢時，更可保平安。
圖左：中央留有小孔的蛙型枕可令側睡小孩的耳朵不致被壓着。

Some stuffed pillows made by mothers for their children were filled with buckwheat husks to maintain extra dryness for the pillow and rectify the shape of the infant's head.
Right: A double-headed tiger pillow from Shijiazhuang of Hebei Province. This shape protected the sleeping child from devils and nightmares.
Left: A frog pillow with a hole in the centre allowed the child to sleep on his side in comfort without having the ear pressed.

是被視爲天子的象徵，故少用於民間，而鳳凰與鴛鴦常被婦女用作背兒帶上的花紋，寄望婚姻美滿及子孫興旺。以下將分類介紹一些民間常見的例子：

## （一）禽獸類

傳統上，人們相信小孩穿上動物類形的衣飾，可以嚇走邪神惡魔，或騙倒它們以爲兒童祇是一頭野獸。獸鞋更帶給小兒多一雙眼睛，因而可以認清路途。

### 老虎

多見於北方小孩衣飾，包括有虎頭帽、口圍、鞋、小兒虎頭枕以及民間玩具如布虎和叫虎等。老虎生性凶猛，爲獸中之王，老虎額上的紋樣，更與〝王〞字相近，故可辟妖祛邪。但小孩衣飾及玩具上的老虎，造型卻又善良可愛，致令老虎有既凶猛（可保護人）又平易近人的雙重形象。虎又同〝富〞諧音，即寄望孩子大富大貴，如虎般健康壯實。

common images used by embroiderers in the folk community are illustrated as follows:

## (1) Birds, insects and beasts

According to folk belief, children's clothing and footwear, if in the shape of animals, could be used to frighten off malicious spirits or fool the evil spirits into thinking that the infant was only an animal, not a human, and therefore not worth harming. The wearing of animal shoes with bulging eyes further assisted the child in keeping him from tripping as he first learned to walk.

### Tiger

This animal was found mostly in the clothing, headdresses and accessories of children in northern regions and could be seen in items such as tiger hats, collars, shoes and pillows, as well as in folk toys like the rag and roaring tigers. The tiger was believed to be the king of all forest life and the *wang* (king) character was supposedly seen in the stripes on its forehead. Tiger images were popular because tigers were considered not to be particularly inimical to human beings and were fierce enough to frighten away evil spirits. The images of tigers found on children's costumes and toys were especially non-hostile and lovely. The word tiger, *hu*, was a homonym for "wealth" representing the hope for a child to have a prosperous future and the robust health of the tiger.

雞

多見於布縫及泥塑玩具。古以雞有五德,故稱德禽,亦爲六畜之一,可避邪。雞亦與〝吉〞諧音。雄雞每於天亮啼叫,驅走活躍於黑夜的邪魔鬼怪,象徵白晝的開始,雞又能啄食五毒,除去害蟲。

豬

多見於布縫玩具動物、童帽、口圍及鞋,寓意豐足。

貓

多見於童鞋,布縫玩具動物。
貓吃鼠,能保護安睡小兒不被老鼠侵襲。
貓與〝耄〞諧音,七、八十歲稱耄,寓意長壽。

## Rooster

The rooster image was found mostly in rag and clay toys. In ancient Chinese texts, the rooster was believed to possess the "five virtues" and was therefore called "the animal of virtue". The rooster, *ji,* was also a homonym with the word "auspicious". Moreover, the rooster was the symbol of the sun as it crowed when the sun rose. The loud crow of the rooster every morning would scare away the evil spirits or ghosts which were particularly active at night. The rooster also offered protection to the child by capturing the five poisonous creatures and eating insects which might bring sickness.

## Pig

Pigs were found in children's hats, shoes, collars and in the shapes of stuffed toy animals. The image of a pig symbolized "abundance", "richness" and "sumptuousness".

## Cat

Cats were often found on children's shoes and in the shape of stuffed toy animals. Cats caught rats which might attack the infant while he slept. The word cat, *mao*, was a homonym with the word "septuagenarian", a symbol of longevity.

虎 Tiger

雞 Rooster

豬 Pig

貓 Cat

蝶

多見於衣服紋樣，蝶與〝耋〞諧音，八、九十歲稱耋，象徵長壽。

兔

多見於布縫和泥塑玩具如兔兒爺。

兔兒爺的形象來自神話月宮中的嫦娥、玉兔的傳說。玉兔搗藥爲天下人治病驅災，因而可保小孩吉利平安。又因玉兔活上千年，亦寓長壽。

魚

多見於衣飾及獸鞋。

魚與〝餘〞諧音，寓意年年有餘，此外還有魚躍龍門之意。

蝙蝠

多見於衣服紋樣。

蝙與〝福〞諧音，故蝙蝠是多福臨門的象徵。

**Butterfly**

Butterflies were used as motifs on children's clothing. The word butterfly, *die*, was a homonym with the word "octogenarian" which also meant longevity.

**Hare**

Hares, or rabbits, were found mostly in the form of stuffed toy animals and clay toys like the "Gentleman Hare". According to the Chinese legend of the story of the moon, the hare could be seen pounding the elixir of immortality under the cassia tree in the Palace of the Moon. Thus, the folk community believed the hare had the power of curing diseases of the adults and children. Moreover, the legends told that the hare had been living for a thousand years and so became a symbol of longevity.

**Fish**

Fish were found mostly as motifs on children's clothing and shoes. Fish, *yu*, is a homonym with the word for surplus. The carp was a fish that spent its entire life swimming upstream, eventually reaching the Golden Gate. To common people, this meant that they, too, might one day become officials.

**Bat**

The bat was found mostly as a motif on children's costumes. The word bat, *fu*, was a homonym with the word "good fortune". Five bats together symbolized the "five blessings" comprising "longevity", "wealth", "health", "love of virtue" and "natural death".

"兔兒爺" "Gentleman Hare"

蝶 Butterfly

魚 Fish

蝙蝠 Bat

鹿

多見於衣飾紋樣。鹿與〝祿〞諧音，象徵官祿。希望孩子能獲得功名利祿，光宗耀祖。

五毒

多見於兒童衣飾及鞋帽上。五毒是蝎子、蜥蜴、蜈蚣、毒蛇、蟾蜍（或蜘蛛，因地方而異），借此毒蟲以毒攻毒，寓驅病消災之意。

麒麟

多見於衣飾上。相傳麒麟爲仁義之獸，是吉祥的象徵。並可爲不育的婦女帶來兒子，稱爲〝麒麟送子〞。

獅子

多見於民間玩具如布獅、泥獅等。爲除邪祥瑞之獸。

**Deer**

The deer could be found as a motif on children's clothing. The deer, *lu*, signified "wealth" as the word deer was a homonym with the word for the official's salary. It was the desire of every parent that their son become an official and at the same time bring wealth and glory to the family.

**Five Poisons**

The five poisons were employed as embroidery motifs on children's clothing and accessories. The "Five Poisons" included the scorpion, lizard, centipede, snake and toad (or spider; the specific insects vary from region to region). The depiction of these creatures would have the neutralizing effect of using evil against evil, thus offering protection to children against harm and disease.

***Qilin* (Unicorn)**

*Qilin* figured prominently as motifs of children's clothing. Traditionally, the *qilin* was regarded as "the creature of benevolence and righteousness". It was also auspicious in that it brought sons to childless families.

**Lion**

The lion was found mostly in the folk toys like rag and clay lions and patterns on children's clothing. The lion was considered as an auspicious animal that could ward off demons.

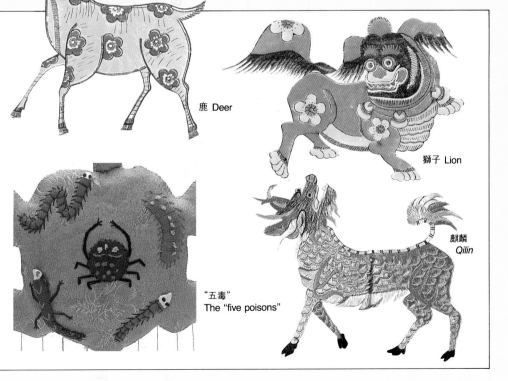

鹿 Deer

獅子 Lion

"五毒"
The "five poisons"

麒麟
*Qilin*

（二）人物及神仙類

仙人或傳說中的主角人物，作為兒童的模範。諸如廿四孝故事或民間傳奇裡的人物，如西遊記的孫悟空、劉海戲蟾故事裡帶給人們財富的劉海……等等，常出現在兒童衣飾及玩具造型上。

八仙

多見於兒童的帽飾，伴著八仙的有壽星或笑佛。此類帽子多流行於浙江及江蘇一帶，華北及西北較罕有。相傳八仙是八位神通廣大的神仙，分別出現於民間傳說如〝八仙過海〞和〝八仙賀壽〞等。他們能消災驅邪，降福給民間老百姓。

壽星

多見於衣飾紋樣，壽星又名南極仙翁，是神話中長壽之神，可保小兒長命百歲。此外還有福星和祿星，象徵福氣、官位及財富。

## (2) Human characters and deities

This category included the immortals as major legendary characters serving as models of goodness for children. For example, the characters of the "Twenty-four Tales of Filial Piety", the Monkey King in the story of "A Journey to the West" and the auspicious character who brought wealth to poor people in the legend of "Liu Hai and the Three-legged Toad" were commonly seen in the embroidery of children's costumes and used as the themes for folk toys.

### Eight Immortals

The Eight Immortals were prominent figures as hat ornaments and amulets accompanied by *Shouxing* (God of Longevity) or the Laughing Buddha. Such caps with the Eight Immortals were typical of the Zhejiang and Jiangsu regions, but were rarely seen in the north or west. The Eight Immortals were believed to be deities who manipulated their extraordinary power to cross the sea, and congratulated the Queen Mother of the West Heavens on her birthday. They were also capable of protecting people from evil forces and of bringing good fortune.

### *Shouxing* (God of Longevity)

The God of Longevity was found as a motif on children's clothing and in the form of amulets used as hat ornaments. *Shouxing* (the Star of Longevity) was regarded as the God of Longevity, able to ensure children's survival and long life. In addition, the *fu* and *lu* stars were symbols of good fortune, officialdom and wealth.

▽
衆八仙和壽星被邀往西王母主持的蟠桃大會
山東省濰縣木刻年畫
Both the Eight Immortals and *Shouxing* (Star of Longevity) were invited to the Grand Peach Ceremony presided over by the Queen Mother of the West Heavens, Xi Wangmu. Woodblock print of Wei County, Shandong Province.

34

八仙圖
山東省濰縣木刻年畫

| 曹國舅 | 藍采和 | 張果老 | 鍾離權 |
| 呂洞賓 | 李鐵拐 | 何仙姑 | 韓湘子 |

The Eight Immortals
Woodblock prints of Wei County, Shandong Province.

| Cao Guojiu | Lan Caihe | Zhang Guolao | Zhong Liquan |
| Lu Dongbin | Li Tieguai | He Xiangu | Han Xiangzi |

35

▽
石榴、佛手瓜、蝙蝠和桃的組合象徵多子、多福和長壽。天津楊柳青木刻年畫。
The combination of the pomegranate, "melon of the Buddha's hand", bat and peach together symbolizes fertility, good fortune and longevity. Woodblock print of Yangliuqing, Tianjin, Hebei Province.

## （三）植物類

多寓意代代興旺,不斷繁衍及子孫滿堂。

### 蓮花及其他花卉圖案

蓮花多爲小兒口圍的形狀及衣飾花紋等。蓮與〝連〞同音,而蓮子的子,則表示孩子,即爲連生貴子之意。其他花卉圖案如牡丹,象徵富貴燦爛,多用來填補和裝飾刺繡品上空餘的地方。

### 石榴

多見於小兒衣飾紋樣,果內種子甚多,民間用來寓多子,如〝榴生百子〞。

### 瓜

見於衣飾紋樣。瓜的種子多,〝瓞〞是小瓜。瓜瓞綿綿比喻子孫繁衍興盛,綿綿不絕,而佛手瓜的佛手更與〝福壽〞諧音。

## (3) Plants

Plants of all kinds were used as symbols of fertility, meaning abundance of offspring.

### Lotus and other floral patterns

The lotus flower was widely employed as the shape of children's collars, and as a motif on clothing. The lotus, *lian*, was a homonym for "continually". The seeds of the lotus were called *lian zi* when *zi* referred to seeds or sons. The whole idea would, then, be of continually producing sons. Other floral patterns, such as the peony, symbolized prosperity.

### Pomegranate

Mostly found as a motif on children's clothing, the pomegranate was full of seeds and therefore used by the mothers to represent their desire for sons.

### Melon

Mostly found as a motif on children's clothing, the melon with its countless seeds represented families' hopes for sons. A kind of citrus fruit called "the melon of the Buddha's hand" was considered to be auspicious since the words Buddha, *fo*, and hand, *shòu*, were two homonyms for the words "good luck" and "longevity".

### Gourd

Gourds were found mostly as motifs on children's clothing. One style of children's *dudou* (apron) was in a shape combining the features of a gourd and a peach. The two Chinese characters for gourd, *hulu*, formed a homonym for the words "good fortune" and "wealth". Besides having a great number of seeds, the gourd resembled the shape of a

### 葫蘆

多見於衣飾紋樣,小兒肚兜其中一款形狀亦介乎葫蘆與桃之間。葫蘆與〝福祿〞諧音,亦爲多子的果實,其形狀有如懷孕的婦女,寓意子孫昌盛。葫蘆又是古代郎中裝藥的器皿,故亦有祛除疾病的寓意。

### 桃

多見於衣飾紋樣,傳說西王母有蟠桃園,仙桃三千年開花、三千年結果,食之長生不老,故象徵長壽。

## (四)其他

### 爆竹

小孩玩意,爆竹聲嚇走鬼怪。爆竹內的硫磺硝烟,有驅瘟除疫及消毒作用。

### 花燈

燈與〝丁〞諧音,比喻〝添丁〞。民間不育女子有偷燈習俗,取其意頭。

pregnant woman, thus further symbolized fertility. Moreover, gourds were used by traditional herbalists as receptacles to hold medicine which offered protection to children against diseases.

### Peach

Peaches appeared as motifs on children's clothing as symbols of longevity. According to legend, the Queen Mother of the West Heavens owned a great orchard where the peach blossoms flowered every three thousand years and the fruit matured after another three thousand years.

## (4) Others

### Firecracker

A kind of game for children, firecrackers were set off for protective purposes. The sound produced would frighten off the evil spirits, whilst the sulphur released controlled the proliferation of plagues and pestilences by killing harmful bacteria.

### Lantern

The lantern, *ding*, was a homonym with the word "son", symbolizing the giving birth to a son. The custom of "stealing the lantern" was supposed to bring sons to childless families.

### Coin

Found mainly as a motif on baby carriers and children's clothing, the coin was a symbol for prosperity and could also be used to ward off evil things.

△

萬事如意圖案

*Ruyi* against a background of *wan* (swastika)

▷

象徵財富的古錢圖案常見於背兒帶的紋樣中

A close-up of the patchwork "coin" pattern on a traditional baby carrier. The pattern symbolizes wealth.

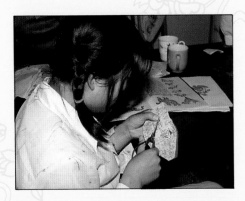

△

陝西省洛川縣婦女在剪製剪紙，剪紙又可作為刺繡的底樣。

A woman working on papercuts, Luochuan County, Shaanxi Province.
Papercuts sometimes served as stencils to assist in embroidery work.

### 古錢

見於背兒帶上或其他小兒衣服飾樣。
古錢可驅邪及喻意財富。

### 如意及萬字紋

見於衣飾紋樣，與古錢等多用來填補和裝飾刺繡品上空餘的地方。並喻萬事如意。

### *Ruyi* and *wan* (swastika)

These two decorative patterns were embroidered on clothing. Similar to the floral patterns and "coin", the *ruyi* and *wan* patterns were frequently used to fill the vacant spaces of the embroideries, making the overall design more interesting. The word *wan* meant "ten thousand", or "infinity", and *wan* and *ruyi* together meant that everything one wished would be obtained.

# 兒童玩藝
# Amusements: Toys and Games

五 花八門的玩具,不僅能豐富兒童的生活,還能促進兒童的智力發展,陶冶性情。雖然中國民間玩具的歷史久遠,但一直以來乏人重視,因此有關它的歷史,在文獻中記載不多。據李寸松先生在談論我國玩具起源時提出,在新石器時代河姆渡文化出土的雙首陶豬,以及仰韶文化西安半坡遺址出土的石球、陶球和陶塤(一種吹奏樂器),大抵是我國最早出現的玩具雛形。其後在漢、唐、宋及清各朝的墓葬中,亦發現過兒童所用之陶、瓷器玩具。

根據史籍記載和繪畫所見,我國早期的傳統玩具包括有撥浪鼓、陀螺、不倒翁、風箏和泥人…等,其中有些出現於漢代以前,甚至作爲商品行銷於市。(可參考宋,李嵩之《貨郎圖》)早在周朝,在楚國人老萊子的《戲彩娛親》中,已經提到當時的一種玩具,名爲"撥浪鼓",是由古代的禮器"鞉"演化而成。形如小鼓,有柄,兩旁繫珠墜,持柄轉動時,珠墜自擊鼓而發聲。

▽
根據古籍記載,早在周朝,楚國人老萊子已用"撥浪鼓"娛樂雙親。

*Bolanggu* were mentioned in ancient texts as toys used by Lao Laizi, a man of the Zhou Dynasty, for entertaining his parents.

戲彩娛親

W hile children are most fascinated by the variety of and pleasure provided by toys, toys also facilitate children's intellectual growth and nurturing of sentiments. Despite the long history of toys in the Chinese folk community, they were seldom viewed as of great significance, nor were they mentioned in historical accounts. According to Mr. Li Cunsong's study of the origin of toys in China, the double-headed pottery pig unearthed from the Hemudu Culture of the neolithic period, the stone and pottery balls and pottery *xun* (ocarina) excavated from the site of Banpo (Xian) of the Yangxiao Culture could all be considered as prototypes of toys in China. Children's toys made of pottery and porcelain were discovered among the tomb finds of subsequent dynasties: for example, Han, Tang, Song and Qing.

As can be traced from certain historical records and paintings, traditional varieties of Chinese toys from earlier eras included *bolanggu* (a drum-shaped rattle), tops, tumblers (roly-polys), kites, claymen etc. These items were for sale in the markets as early as prior to the Han Dynasty. The *bolanggu*, mentioned in ancient texts as toys used by Lao Laizi of the Zhou Dynasty for entertaining his parents, was

△
近代之不倒翁,陝西及華北地區。
Modern tumblers, Shaanxi Province and North China.

◁
陀螺,廣東省,約一九二〇年代。
A top, Guangdong Province, c.1920's

陀螺爲圓錐體形,上大下小,玩時以繩抽之,置於地上,使它旋轉不停。陀螺可用木、陶、竹或石製。山西夏縣西陰村仰韶文化遺址中,曾出土陶製小陀螺。

不倒翁也叫〝扳不倒兒〞,用泥、木、紙等材料製成老人、娃娃、縣官或動物等各種形象。上輕下重,底部爲半球形。扳倒後能自動豎立,並搖擺轉動。它由唐代的〝酒胡子〞演變而來,原本是於席間飲宴時作爲勸酒所用。

風箏在古代文獻上又稱〝紙鳶〞,最初爲探測天氣、占卜運程和傳達書信的工具,並用於軍事上。至唐代以後,才演變爲玩具。晚唐時,又在風箏添加絲弦或竹笛,使風入發聲如箏,故名風箏。我國的風箏是用細竹紮成骨架,糊上紙張或絲織品,並施彩繪,繫以長綫,利用風力放飛到空中。風箏的種類繁多,禽鳥蟲魚、器物等各種形象,無所不有。

△
香港一羣學生所製的風箏
Kites made by a group of students in Hong Kong

▷
會發聲的風箏,南通,江蘇省。
A kite with a sound—producing device, Nantong, Jiangsu Province.

40

derived from a kind of musical instrument in ancient China. *Bolanggu* was a toy made in the shape of a small drum, with a handle and two strings, each with beads attached, which were then fastened, one to a side, at each side of the drum. When the toy was rotated by the handle, the beads would beat on the drum and produce a rattling sound.

A top was a toy in a conical shape, usually symmetrical having a large head and a pointed base. A cord was twined round the spindle and pulled sharply to set the top in motion, usually played on the surface of the ground. Tops were made of wood, clay, bamboo or even stone. Tiny pottery tops were also unearthed in Xiyin village in the site of the Yangxiao Culture in Xia County of Shanxi Province.

Clay, wood and papier mache were the ingredients most commonly used to make the Chinese-type tumblers in the various shapes of old men, babies, officials and animals. These little toys had a weight in the semi-spherical base and however hard they were pushed over, they rolled back to an upright position. Tumbler toys were believed to be derived from the *jiuhuzi*, a Tang Dynasty device for encouraging guests to drink alcohol during feasts.

Kites were historically called *zhiyuan* and were first designed for forecasting the weather, fortelling good or bad luck, communicating messages and observing military operations. It was only after the Tang Dynasty that their use became widespread and kites were flown for fun. Towards the end of the Tang Dynasty, silk strings or bamboo pipes were fitted onto the

唐宋兩代的小孩墓葬還出土過小型瓷質玩具及大批泥製玩具。明代晚期，江蘇省無錫市惠山附近出現了著名的泥人〝阿福〞，成爲我國泥娃娃的表表者。至於古代的玩具，還包括有明代的〝蘭陵面具〞（用紙或木料製成的面具）、布布噠、太平鼓及空竹……等等。益智的玩具則有〝九連環〞和〝七巧板〞。〝九連環〞是由九個圓形金屬環套在橫板或框架上，貫以環柄，掌握一定程序後即可分合。〝七巧板〞是由七塊薄板組成，合起來成正方形，分拆後可以排成各種事物圖形。

泥人〝阿福〞，無錫，江蘇省。
The clayman *A Fu,* Wuxi, Jiangsu Province.

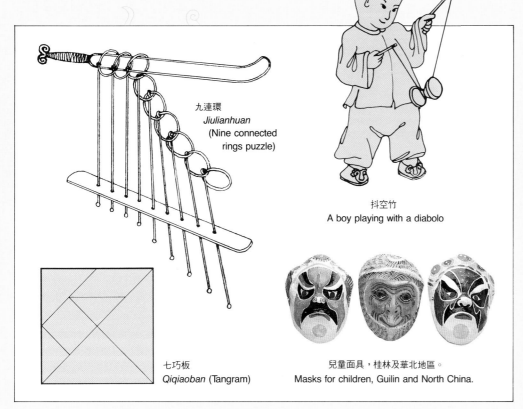

九連環
*Jiulianhuan*
(Nine connected rings puzzle)

抖空竹
A boy playing with a diabolo

七巧板
*Qiqiaoban* (Tangram)

兒童面具，桂林及華北地區。
Masks for children, Guilin and North China.

kite for producing the sound of a zither when a strong wind passed. Hence the name "wind zither" came to refer to all kites, with or without musical instruments attached. Traditional Chinese kites were generally made by stretching richly-decorated paper or silk on bamboo frames with tassels or tails attached to trail after them. Chinese kites came in every imaginable shape and size such as flowers, insects, animals and figures.

Miniature porcelain toys and a multitude of pottery toys were discovered in the tombs of children during both the Tang and Song Dynasties. In the late Ming Dynasty, one of the most well known types of playthings in China, the clayman *A Fu* (the lucky one) was first produced in the neighourhood of Huishan in Wuxi in Jiangsu Province. *A Fu* then became the masterpiece of clay figurines in Chinese history. Moreover, playthings from the early periods also included the *lanling* facemask of the Ming Dynasty, made of paper and bits of wood, and the *kongzhu* (diabolo). In addition, Chinese puzzles such as the *jiulianhuan* (the Nine Connected Rings puzzle) and the *qiqiaoban* (Tangram) enjoyed great popularity as challenges to people's skills. The Nine Connected Rings puzzle was comprised of nine metal rings mysteriously attached to a loop fitted into a handle (as shown in the diagram). The object of the puzzle was to remove all nine rings from the loop – an operation which involved many different manipulations. The tangram was a thin square cut into seven pieces which could then be arranged to form the outlines of countless different objects such as fish, birds, animals and people.

41

綜合來說，鄉土玩具所採納的題材多與民間生活息息相關。製造的原料亦非常簡單，不外乎是泥、紙、布、竹、草、木或石等等。加上了鮮艷的顏色，除了在視覺上吸引外，有時還可發聲，令兒童愛不釋手。昔日，除了有貨郎挑擔子在街上叫賣玩具外，每逢臨近年節或廟會的日子，鄉間農民更趕製大批玩具在市集出售，加添節日的熱鬧氣氛。

中國的玩具除了帶給我國千萬兒童無窮的歡欣喜悅外，還流傳到海外。例如古老的智力遊戲〝七巧板〞，曾傳到世界各地，在國外稱爲〝唐圖〞，意爲〝中國的圖板〞。而在日本的博物館，曾陳列了在奈良時代由中國傳入的〝撥浪鼓〞。此外，民間的玩偶只限於外型較簡單的紙、泥或瓷製的〝像人〞玩具，絕少加上立體的五官或毛髮。相信這是基於民間信仰及禁忌，認爲神肖而附以四肢及衣服的〝人〞像，有超自然能力，故多置於神廟裡供人膜拜。另

Generally speaking, the themes of folk toys were closely related to daily practices in the folk community. Though gorgeously painted and vividly coloured, these traditional playthings were made of simple raw materials- clay, paper, cloth, bamboo, straw, wood and stone. Besides the toy's immediate visual impact, special devices were added for producing the sound effects that best explained the children's fondness for toys. In former days, toy pedlars were occasionally found wandering the streets, carrying baskets of toys on their shoulder poles. When the times for traditional festivals and temple gatherings were near, both villagers and merchants who knew the art would manufacture and assemble large quantities of toys to be sold in the markets.

Traditional Chinese toys not only filled the Chinese children's world with joy and excitement, but also were spread wide, even to overseas countries. For instance, the tangram has been found all over the world with the name "The Board of the Tang Dynasty", meaning "The Board of China". The *bolanggu* of the Nara period, once displayed in a museum in Japan, also provided evidence of the spread of Chinese toys into Japan in the early years. More interesting is the absence of the concept of "doll" in the traditional Chinese folk community. Playthings nearest to this idea were limited to those human-like toy figures such as claymen, in simple design and made of paper, pottery or porcelain. Three dimensional facial features were seldom added although the five sense organs (the eyes, nose and ears etc) and hair were painted onto the faces and heads of the claymen. According to folk belief, those realistic human – like figures, given four limbs and dressed like

△ 成人及兒童在街頭觀看木偶戲，十九世紀。
Children and adults watching puppet show in the street, 19th century.

▽ 兒童踩高蹺，天津楊柳青木刻年畫。
Children walking on stilts, woodblock print of Yangliuqing, Tianjin, Hebei Province.

外亦迷信神肖的造像，若被仇家帶走，可加以符咒，而致自身受害。直到十九世紀，我國才製造一些耳目、四肢精巧，配以華美服飾的娃娃，但多半是出口到西方國家，供海外成人或兒童玩賞。

近百年來，民間玩具亦不斷發展，造型生動活潑，品種繁多。例如河北、山東、陝西各省出產的泥娃娃和泥獸等。此外，還有布縫和竹製玩具、積木，甚至泥餑餑模子、萬花筒和刀槍劍戟……等。可是，玩具對於精力充沛的兒童來說，仍未能盡興。他們還創思出花款繁多的各種遊戲方式，好像是捉迷藏、老鷹捉小雞、放風箏、放花炮、鬥蟋蟀、踢毽子、騎竹馬、提花燈、弄皮影、轉風車、翻綾、溜冰、打彈珠、扮媳婦、學唱戲……等等。

men, were regarded as having magical and supernatural powers. They were kept only in temples as ritual objects for people's worship. It was also believed that, if the human-like figures in a private collection were unfortunately stolen by an enemy and given charms, the owner would suffer bodily harm. It was not until the 19th century that China designed and manufactured true "dolls" neatly and elaborately dressed in Chinese style, with detailed facial features and separate limbs. However, the majority of these dolls were exported to western countries for the amusement of adults and children.

During the last hundred years, folk toys have undergone a series of changes, attaining their present rich content and great variety. In addition to the claymen and clay animals manufactured in the Provinces of Hebei, Shandong and Shaanxi, there are rag stuffed toys, toy building blocks, bamboo-made toys, toy clay moulds, kaleidoscopes and toy weapons. However, more energetic children find even these various kinds of toys insufficient for utmost enjoyment, and they have had to invent their games out of nothing. Throughout the ages, children have devised new games too many to number. For example: hide-and-seek, tug of war, the old eagle snatches the little chicks, kite-flying, the lighting of fireworks, cricket fighting, shuttlecock kicking, bamboo-horse riding, lantern carrying, shadow puppets, playing cat's cradle, ice-skating, playing marbles, marriage games, and acting out opera pieces.

會發聲的玩具
Toys that produce sounds

積木，約一九六〇年代。
Building blocks, c. 1960's

泥塑及木製玩具
Clay and wooden toys

▷
布縫玩具動物
Stuffed toy animals

△
鬃人，北京
爲泥、紙或綢布造成的戲裝小人，足下黏上一圈豬鬃毛。玩時把鬃人放在銅盤裡，用木棍輕震盤邊，鬃人即會旋轉及行走等。

*Zongren,* Beijing
A kind of folk toy constructed of clay, paper or silk fabric and made in the shape of an operatic character standing on a ring of pig's bristles. During play, the *zongren* was placed in a copper basin and would rotate and move about when the basin was given a thump.

▷
各類竹、泥及紙製玩具

Toys made of bamboo, clay and paper

△
民間兒童遊戲，清代《吳友如畫寶》
老鷹捉小雞　拍球　踢毽子
翻筋斗　捉迷藏　擲錢遊戲

△
Children at play, from *Wu Youru hua bao*, Qing.
The old eagle snatches the little chicks　Playing ball　Kicking a shuttlecock
Turning somersaults　Hide and seek　The rolling of coins

△

民間兒童遊戲，清代《吳友如畫寶》

| 鬥蟋蟀 | 騎牛（馬）遊戲 | 放風箏 |
| 賞金魚 | 玩樂器 | 提花燈 |

△

Children at play, from *Wu Youru hua bao*, Qing.

Cricket fighting      Playing piggyback

Having fun with goldfish      Playing musical instruments

Kite flying

Carrying lanterns

# 中國傳統兒童服飾
# DRESS AND SYMBOLISM IN CHINA

嘉麗 Valery M. Garrett

# 童 服
# Children's Clothing

中國是一個傳統的農業社會，大部份人民居住在農村裏，在衛生環境還沒有改善、醫療服務還沒有普及以前，兒童的死亡率是十分高的，有很多甚至活不到一歲。在傳統中國社會裏，一般父母都希望百子千孫，養育多些兒女，除了因為兒童死亡率極高外，還有一個重要原因，尤其是在較貧窮的家庭裏，多些兒女能增加家庭的勞動力，以協助父母從事農耕及漁獵等活動。傳統中國社會不單止着重大家庭，更着重是否有男丁繼後香燈，亦只有男丁才可參加科舉考試，能金榜提名的話，便可以光宗耀祖，為家族帶來財富與榮譽。

傳統上，中國人普遍相當迷信，因此往往在兒童的衣服上繡上花卉、水果、動物及昆蟲紋樣，用來保護兒童，驅走鬼怪。代表幸運、財富和長壽的福、祿、壽三星更常繡於兒童衣服上。兒童日常多穿着棉質衣服，在某些特別日子才會穿絲質或緞質之衣服，顏色多是鮮艷的如紅色、粉紅色等，寓意吉祥。

## 嬰兒服裝
嬰兒出生後，會被父母用一塊由家庭其他成員的衣服所造成的包布包裹着。嬰兒及母親在嬰兒出生後一個月內都會足不出戶。直至嬰兒滿月，家庭才會設宴慶祝。這時候嬰兒的包布會被除去，

China was always predominantly an agricultural society, where the majority of people lived in the countryside. In the past, before hygiene improved and medical care became more easily available, a child in China had a very high mortality rate, with large numbers not surviving to their first birthday. It was the ambition of parents to have a large family for several reasons: for the poorer families sons were needed to help in the fields or when fishing, while for others, sons who did well in the Imperial examinations brought wealth and distinction to the clan. Furthermore, sons were needed to ensure the continuation of the clan, as well as to perform the very necessary ritual ceremonies of ancestor worship.

Consequently, superstition was rife, and a child's clothing was covered in flowers, fruit, animals and insects, each endowed with protective properties to ward off evil, as well as to bring the child great success in the future. The three most popular mythological figures, Fuk, Luk and Shou, standing for luck, an abundance of good things, and long life were also depicted on many articles of dress. Cotton was used for everyday wear, with richly embroidered silks and satins for special

改爲穿着由祖母親手縫製的一套紅綠色衣服，包括一件上衣、一件背心、一條開襠褲、一件肚兜及一頂帽子。

在上一世紀，母親還需要親手縫造一件衣服給嬰兒，名爲「百家衣」。由親友們各自送出一小幅布料，母親把這些布料縫起來，便成衣服。其用意是由親友們每人都爲嬰兒作福，祈求平安。

嬰兒滿月後，便要選擇吉日進行剃頭。他們認爲新生的頭髮會更濃密和健康，這可防止日後脫髮。幾個月後會再有另一次剃頭，這次頭頂的頭髮會被剃去，剩下兩撮頭髮在耳朵對上的部位，又或許會繞着頭頂剃剩一圈頭髮。這樣做的原因是希望在嬰兒遇到邪魔或危險時，父母能抓着他們的頭髮拯救他們。人們相信剃去所有頭髮是不祥的。

▷
女童髮式，十九世紀末。
Young girls' hairstyles, late 19th century.
(Headland I.T. *Chinese Mother Goose Rhymes,* pub. 1900)

occasions. Colours were bright, and reds and pinks were frequently used because these were considered to be auspicious.

## Babies and Young Children

When a child was born it would be washed and then wrapped in swaddling clothes, generally made from cast-off clothing of other family members. Neither the child, nor its mother, would venture out of doors until the end of the first month after the birth, at which time a celebratory feast would be held for family and friends. At this point, sets of red and green clothing, tailored along the same lines as their parents, and comprising of a centre opening jacket or a *sam* (a jacket fastening over to the right side), a waistcoat, divided trousers, navel cover and hat would be presented by the maternal grandmother to replace the swaddling clothes.

At this time other gifts were bestowed on the child. One common tradition during the last century was that of giving the mother small pieces of silk and embroidery for her to sew together to make the child a jacket. This was known as a "Hundred Families Coat", and all those who contributed joined in wishing the child good fortune and protection from evil.

Cutting a child's hair was governed by superstition and when the baby was almost a month old a lucky day was chosen for shaving the head. This was said to make the real crop grow thicker and to prevent it from falling out in later life. At a second shaving some months later, the crown was shaved but two circular

嬰兒滿月家人會再設宴慶祝，父母會給他們穿着漂亮的衣服，包括絲質繡花上衣及開襠褲。開襠褲已有數百年歷史。嬰兒之內衣主要有遮臍布及肚兜。事實上直至三至四歲前，小童在炎夏也多只穿肚兜。

## 男童

一般人對於男孩子能否受教育是非常重視的，能夠接受教育便可以參加科舉考試，藉以光宗耀祖。很多富有人家會聘請老師教導其子女，有些村莊會設立私塾或書室栽培其村的子弟。男孩子在七歲開始便要背誦「三字經」、「論語」、「易經」等。較少接觸地理、科學等學科。

三歲、四歲開始，男孩子穿着長衫，多是灰色或藍色絲質，長及腳踝部份，右邊扣鈕。平常他們也會在長衫上再穿一件背心。背心有緄邊及繡滿

sections of hair, one above each ear, or even a whole ring was left around the bald spot. On no account must the tufts be removed or the child would meet with an untimely death. Furthermore, it was to enable the parents to seize the tufts when the child was in danger of being whisked away by bad spirits!

The child's first birthday was a time for another great feast. The child would be dressed in a silk embroidered jacket, either centre-fastening or side-fastening. This was worn together with embroidered divided trousers consisting of two pieces of cloth attached to a broad waistband, and joined from ankle to knee leaving the area covering the buttocks free. This style of trousers dates back hundreds of years and is illustrated in a children's reader first published in 1436.

△
嬰兒一歲生日。左邊的男童穿長衫馬褂，在母親膝上的幼兒頭戴繡繪了花紋的帽，身穿外衣和長褲；右邊的男童則穿長衫和背心。約一九一五年。

Baby's first birthday. The boy on the left is wearing the *cheung sam ma kua*, the baby on his mother's knee wears an embroidered cap, jacket and trousers, while the boy on the right wears the *pui sum* over his *cheung sam*; c. 1915.
(Copyright: V.M. Garrett)

▷
中國學童，約一八七二年。

Chinese schoolboys, c. 1872
(Worswick C. and Spence J., *Imperial China: Photographs 1850-1912*, New York, 1978.)

彩色花紋。比較年長的男孩在農曆新年或其他特別日子會在長衫外穿藍緞側面扣鈕背心。富有家庭之男孩則流行在長衫外加穿馬褂，以示隆重。馬褂爲一中間扣鈕之黑色緞質外套，與成人所穿的相似。

△
男童穿着背心和長衫。十九世紀末。
Young boy wearing a decorated waistcoat and *cheung sam;* late 19th century.
(Headland I.T. *Chinese Mother Goose Rhymes,* pub. 1900)

▷
清朝最後一個皇帝，溥儀（站立者）兩歲時穿着長衫馬褂。旁邊是他的父親醇親王和弟弟溥傑，一九〇八年。
The last emperor of the Qing dynasty, Pu Yi (standing), age 2, wearing *cheung sam ma kua,* with his father Prince Chun and his brother Pu Jie; 1908.
(Bland J.O.P. and Backhouse E., *China under the Empress Dowager,* pub. 1914.)

Underwear for a young child would consist of the navel cover and later, a small triangular embroidered apron called a *tou tou,* which fastened with tapes round the neck and waist. Indeed, this apron was often the only form of clothing worn by a child in the hot summer months until it was three or four years old.

## Older Boys

Education and literacy were greatly prized, and from an early age boys were groomed to take the Imperial examinations, success in which, it was hoped, would bring wealth and honour to the clan. Families employed private tutors to educate their sons, or else the clan would establish a private school or study hall in order to educate prospective candidates. From the age of seven boys were taught to memorize such essential school primers as the "Three Character Classic", the "Analects of Confucius", and the "Book of Changes". Reciting from memory to the teacher was known as "backing the book", and a boy could grow up learning little of geography, science, mathematics, etc.

From the age of three or four boys wore the *cheung sam* like their fathers. This was a long gown falling staight from the shoulders, reaching to the ankle, fastening down the right side and made of grey or blue silk. Over this, for casual wear, would be worn a side-fastening waistcoat, colourfully embroidered and edged with braid. Older boys wore a blue sleeveless satin waistcoat, side-fastening, known as a *pui sum* over their *cheung sam* at Lunar New Year and on special occasions, but it became increasingly common, in wealthier families, to wear the *ma kua* with the *cheung sam* for formal events.

較年長的女童

傳統上女孩子不需要接受正式教育，她們只需要在家裏幫手做家務，及照顧弟妹。年紀小小的時候便要學習刺繡。藉以縫造家庭所需用品及幫補家計。

在上世紀女孩子都穿斜襟的衫及褲，她們不穿裙，因為裙是已婚婦女才穿的。再者，家境富裕的婦女所穿衣服的繡工，非常精細，衣服亦會有很多裝飾。

一九二〇年代隨着西方思想的傳入，婦女亦得以解放。婦女摒棄以往笨重之衣服而改穿較輕便之長衫。當時青婦女開始穿裙，較年長的則多穿長衫，但腰部收窄，中袖，長衫長及小腿。不同時代有不同之款式，時至今日，香港仍有很多學校以長衫為校服的。

△
母親與三名兒女。左邊的兒子在長衫外再穿一件背心；幼子在後；右邊的女兒穿着長褲子，在外面加上繡有花紋的衫和背心。香港，十九世紀末。

Mother with her three children: on the left, her son wearing a waistcoat over his *cheung sam;* behind him, a younger son; on the right, her daughter wearing a waistcoat over an embroidered *sam,* worn over trousers. Caine Road, Hong Kong, late 19th century.
(Urban Council, Hong Kong Museum of History)

▷
三名女童與一名婦人。坐着的女童穿上衣和半截裙，即女裝長衫的前身。一九二〇年代初。

Three girls with an older woman. The girl seated is wearing a *sam* and skirt, the forerunner to the female *cheung sam;* early 1920's.
(Copyright: V.M. Garrett)

This was a short black satin jacket, with the centre opening fastening with loops and buttons, modelled on that worn by the men.

## Older Girls

Girls were not given any formal education. They were expected to help around the house and with the younger children if the family did not have servants. They were taught to embroider from an early age, both to provide the many articles needed within the family, as well as in some cases, to contribute to the family income.

During the last century girls wore the side-fastening *sam* and trousers cut along the same lines as their mothers, but without the skirt which was the prerogative of the married woman. These garments were often heavily embroidered and very bulky: as the fabrics and embroidery took a long time to produce, generously-cut garments were an indication of the wealth and prestige of the family.

The 1920's were a period of western influence in fashions, and coupled with greater emancipation for women, this resulted in the development of the female *cheung sam* to replace the cumbersome styles worn during the last century. Young girls now began to wear dresses, with a shaped waist and which fastened down the centre back. Older girls wore the *cheung sam* like their mothers, which was slightly fitted at the waist with 3/4 length sleeves, and reached to mid calf, although lengths and details varied in accordance with the fashion of the time. It was also adopted by many schools as uniform and continues to be worn today in some schools in Hong Kong.

## 在節日穿的衣服

在傳統節日如農曆新年時，男童會穿長衫馬褂，香港的鶴佬人則仍保持其一貫衣着風格。鶴佬人源於中國福建，基於其遷移不定生活習慣，他們傳統上較為保守和迷信。鶴佬婦女精於刺繡，她們能為其子女縫造色彩繽紛之背兒帶及帽子。每年農曆五月的大皇爺誕，七歲或以下之鶴佬兒童都穿着黑色背心，背心用顏色鮮艷之布條綑邊，並會佩帶繡工精細，有大量裝飾品之帽及口圍參加慶祝節目。在其他節日及慶典上，鶴佬兒童都會作這些傳統打扮。

## Festival Clothing

Traditional clothing of the *cheung sam ma kua* is occasionally worn by boys at the Lunar New Year. But the group of fishing people in Hong Kong known as Hoklo still preserve their old customs particularly when related to dress. Said to have originated from Fujian province, the Hoklo people are very conservative and superstitious, due in part to their uncertain way of life. The women are prolific embroiderers and make many gaily decorated baby carriers and hats for their young children for daily use throughout the year. At a festival in the fifth lunar month of the year, held to worship their local god *Dai Wong Yeh*, boys and girls up to the age of seven wear black waistcoats trimmed with brightly coloured piping, together with even more elaborately decorated crowns and embroidered collars, in the procession. This traditional dress is also worn at other festivals and celebrations throughout the year.

▷

鶴佬兒童戴上有刺繡紋樣的口圍和飾帶參加大皇爺誕，在旁的祖母替他拿着冠。大埔，香港，一九七九年。

Hoklo children dressed in embroidered collars and sash for the Dai Wong Yeh festival; grandmother holds the crown.
Tai Po, Hong Kong, 1979.
(Garrett V.M., *Traditional Chinese Clothing in Hong Kong and South China*, Oxford University Press, 1987)

**嬰兒套裝**

嬰兒滿月時，祖母親手縫造給嬰兒的一套衣服。香港，約一九五○年。

紅棉質衫，有五顆結鈕。背部近頸處有綠色繩圈作裝飾。

綠棉質背心，有五顆結鈕，背部近頸處有紅色繩圈作裝飾。

白棉質包布，近頸處及腰部有繩圈，用來縛頸和縛腰，固定位置。

紅綠棉質開襠褲，紅腰帶上有繩圈。作為縛腰之用。

### Set of infant's clothes

Set made by child's grandmother for the celebrations held at the first month after the birth.
Hong Kong, c. 1950

Red cotton sam; 5 loop and button fastening. Green loop at back neck, decorative.
37 cm H x 65 cm L

Green cotton sleeveless jacket; 5 loop and button fastening at centre front. Small red decorative loop at back neck.
33 cm W x 32 cm H

White cotton chest wrapper; 2 loops at top for neck ties, centre loop for attaching to waistband ties of trousers; loop and ties at waist.
20 cm H x 46 cm L

Red/green cotton divided trousers; red waistband with loops for ties.
28 cm W x 28 cm H

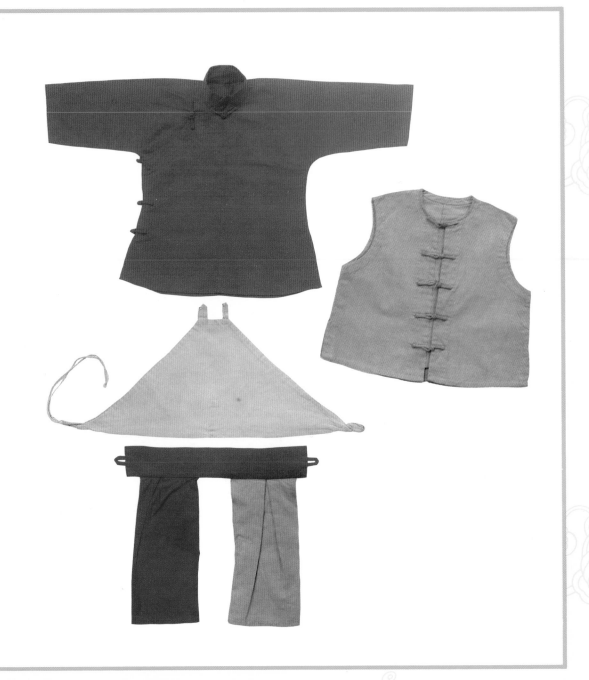

小童「百家衣」。全件衣服由多塊繡有圖案之絲質布幅組成，後幅有縫。十九世紀末。

Child's One Hundred Families jacket, made of several pieces of embroidered silk, lined blue cotton, fringing across back. China, late 19thC.

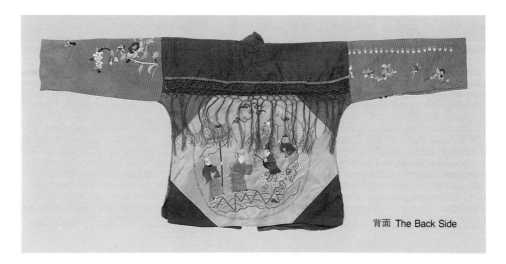

背面 The Back Side

紅緞質女童上衣，衫上用絲線繡上以下圖案：花卉、八仙、壽星、蝙蝠、近頸處有鳳凰。上海，二十世紀初。

Girl's jacket in red satin, embroidered with twisted silk thread and floss silk. Design of flowers and Eight Immortals plus Shou Hsing, a bat and phoenix on the front neckband. Shanghai, early 20thC.
47 cm H x 78 cm L

淡綠緞質開襠褲，用絲線和齊針繡上花卉、鳳凰和兩個分別拿着如意和皮球的小孩。上海，二十世紀初。

Pale green satin divided trousers with satin stitch of twisted silk thread and floss silk embroidery of flowers, phoenix and two dancing children, one holding a *ju-i*, the other a ball. Shanghai, early 20thC.
35 cm W x 46 cm H

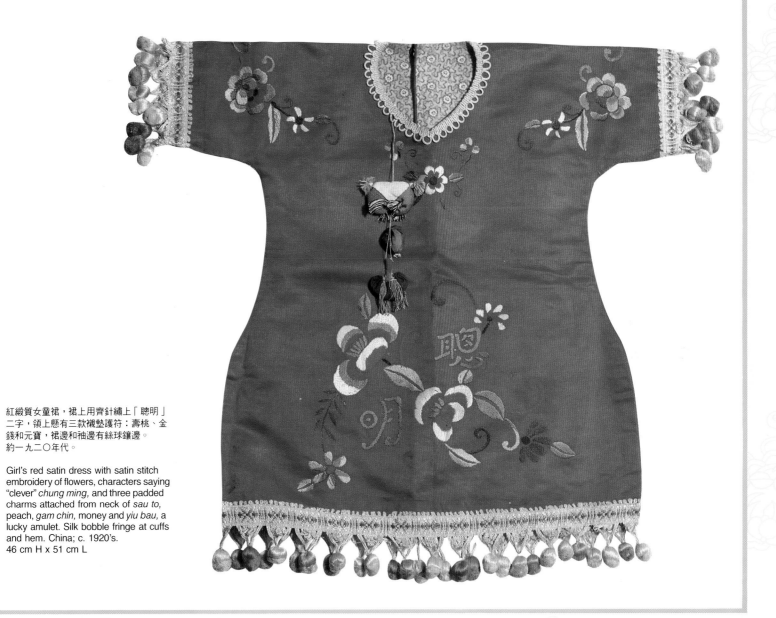

紅緞質女童裙，裙上用齊針繡上「聰明」
二字，領上懸有三款襯墊護符：壽桃、金
錢和元寶，裙邊和袖邊有絲球鑲邊。
約一九二〇年代。

Girl's red satin dress with satin stitch
embroidery of flowers, characters saying
"clever" *chung ming,* and three padded
charms attached from neck of *sau to,*
peach, *gam chin,* money and *yiu bau,* a
lucky amulet. Silk bobble fringe at cuffs
and hem. China; c. 1920's.
46 cm H x 51 cm L

綠緞質兒童肚兜，紫色口袋。繡滿鳳凰、
鹿、獅子、錢幣、花卉等圖案。北京、約
十九世紀。

Child's *toutou* in green satin with purple
satin pocket, appliqued and
embroidered phoenix, deer and lion,
coin, flowers etc. Beijing c. 19thC.
27.5 cm W x 34.5 cm H

黑緞質兒童肚兜，藍棉線及編帶絪邊，用
絲線繡出一隻老虎，四週則有五毒、靈芝
和花卉等圖案。十九世紀末。

Child's *toutou* of black satin lined blue
cotton; edged braid. Floss silk
embroidery depicting a tiger surrounded
by the Five Poisons and the Sacred
Fungus, and flowers. China, late 19thC.
31 cm W x 38 cm H

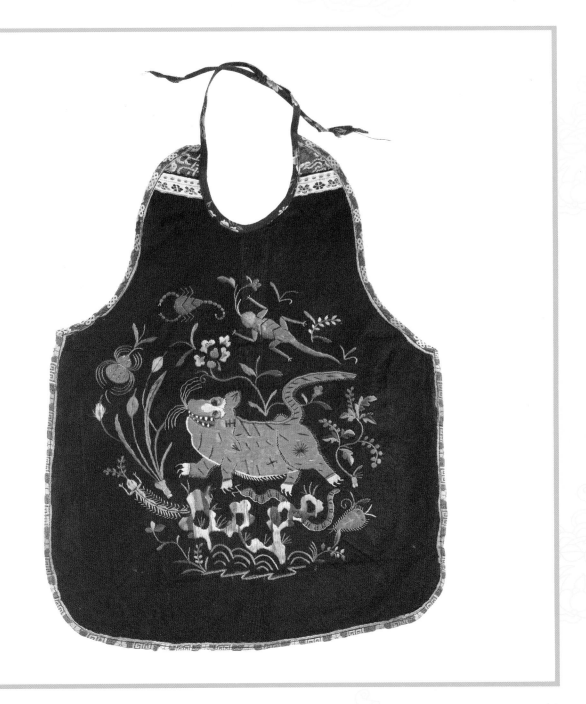

淡紫緞質斜襟女童衫，在腋下打結，衫上用平金法繡上被火焰、花卉和萬字紋圍繞之七隻獅子。上海，約二十世紀初。

Lilac satin *sam* with gold and silver couched embroidery of seven lions surrounded by flames, flowers and the swastika. Lined pink cotton, fastening with ties at underarm. Shanghai, c. early 20thC.
50 cm H x 68 cm L

藍綠緞質開襠褲，用平金法繡上花卉，腰部用粉紅棉布造。上海，約二十世紀初。

Blue/green satin divided trousers with gold and silver couched embroidery of flowers. Lined pink cotton; waistband of pink cotton. Shanghai, c. early 20thC.
41 cm W x 52 cm H

兒童背心，用木梳套針法繡上鳳凰、牡丹花、靈芝和如意。十九世紀。

Child's waistcoat covered in silk embroidery; brick stitch design of phoenix, peony, sacred fungus and *ju-i*; China; 19thC.
39 cm W x 32 cm H

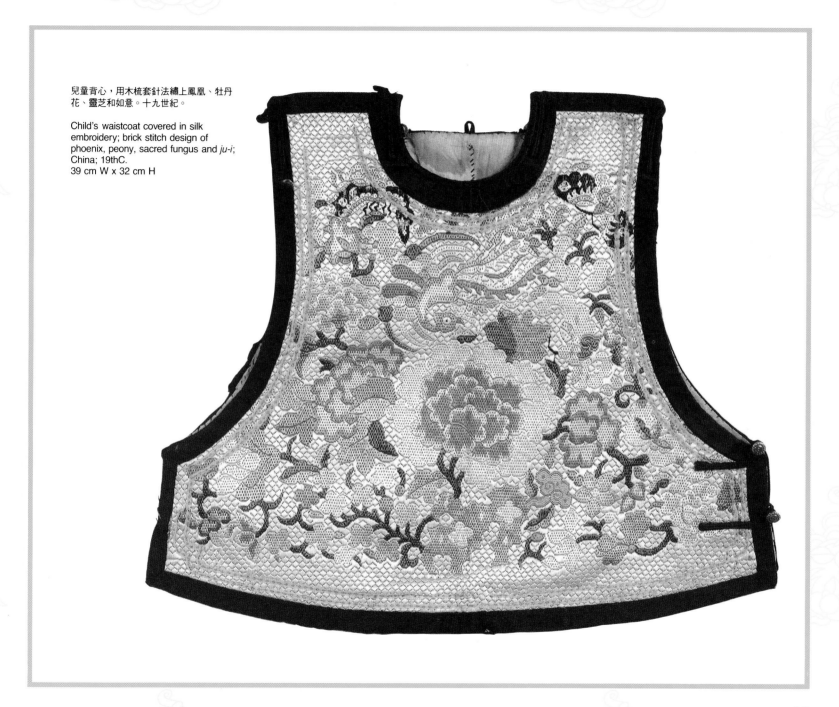

黑絲質男童馬褂，有五顆結鈕。香港，約
一九三〇年。

Boy's black silk jacquard *ma kua;* 5
button and loop fastening, lined blue
silk; Hong Kong, c. 1930.
32 cm H x 73 cm L

鶴佬兒童黑棉質上衣，用彩色棉布條及鎖繡針法鑲邊。有金屬鈕扣，沙頭角，香港，約一九六〇年代。

Hoklo child's black cotton jacket edged with multi coloured cotton piping and decorated with coloured chain stitch embroidery. Loops and embossed metal button fastening at centre front. Shataukok. Hong Kong, c. 1960's. 33 cm W x 40 cm H

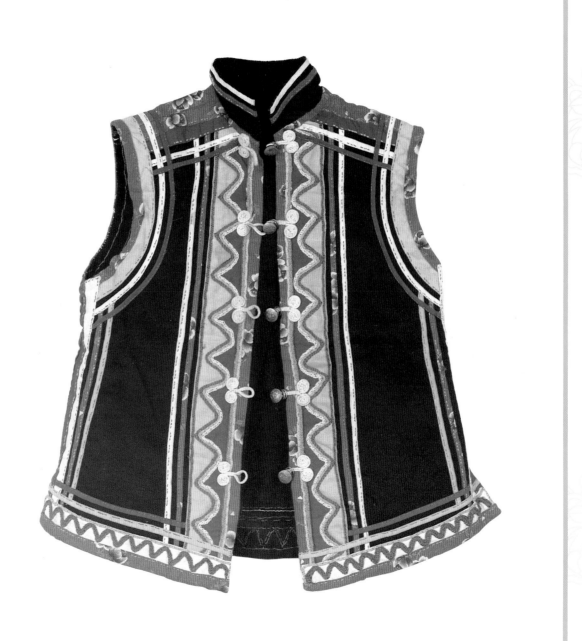

# 背兒帶
# Baby Carriers

母親背嬰兒是中國傳統習俗之一，尤其是在華南一帶。由於大部份的婦女無論在田裏、船上或家裏都需要工作，因此把嬰兒背在背上是最安全的。當家裏的女童長大後，這責任便落在她們身上，由她們照顧弟妹。現在香港新界仍有人使用傳統的背兒帶，近年來始有人採用西方的方法，將嬰兒放在前面。

背兒帶主要是一塊正方形的布，上繡圖案，四角各有一長布條。當嬰兒被背兒帶包着放在母親背上後，兩條布條會越過肩頭放到前面，另外兩條布條穿過腋下放在前面，這樣四條布條便在胸前打結。每條背兒帶上方中央處會釘有一個用布摺成的三角形，以前一般有五層厚，現今祇有一層，這三角形是個吉祥的標誌，象徵五福：壽、富、康寧、攸好德、考終命。也是祈求多子的標誌。人們相信除非父母其一已死，否則背兒帶不能反過來使用。

傳統上，背兒帶是祖母在嬰兒滿月時送給嬰兒的，並由祖母親手縫造，亦有是買回來的。在今天的香港，蛋家及鶴佬婦女仍然親手縫造背兒帶，本地及客家婦女則多從市場購買。

Carrying a baby on the mother's back has long been the custom in China, especially in the southern provinces. For any mother, who had by necessity to work in the fields, on the boat, or round the home, it was also a safe and convenient place to keep a child out of mischief. As the family grew, it was then the turn of the older girls to carry the younger siblings on their backs. Traditional style baby carriers are still used in the rural areas of Hong Kong, although recently some mothers are beginning to carry their babies in front in western style carriers.

The traditional baby carrier is made from a square of cloth, usually decorated with embroidery, with four long strips of fabric extending from each corner of the square to form straps. Once the child and carrier are in place on the mother's back, two straps are brought over her shoulders, and two more come under the arms, to tie in a knot in front. At the centre top of the square is a small folded triangular piece of cloth, previously five layers thick, but now normally of only one layer. It was considered to be a lucky charm and originally symbolized the five blessings: wealth, health, happiness, long life, and the right to a natural death. In addition, it was a wish for

## 廣東及客家式

背兒帶大致分爲三大類，第一類爲本地及客家人常使用的，這類背兒帶的布條並不是另外縫於四個角的，而是由背兒帶的正方形布幅所伸延出來的。傳統的背兒帶比現在的較大，正方形邊長五十至六十厘米，布條每條長一百一十厘米。在布條的尾部有一小袋可盛銅錢，背兒帶大多爲棉或麻質，顏色有紫、黑及深藍色，其中央有絲或絨線所繡之花紋；也有空白沒有繡花的。現在的背兒帶較爲簡單，用紅或印花棉布造成。在某些特別場合或日子，也有用紅色緞布或織錦造成的背兒帶。

在背兒帶上之花紋圖案多數是寓意吉祥的。最常見的有以下的組合：代表婚姻忠誠的鴛鴦、代表富足的石榴、代表純潔的蓮花、代表夫婦和諧及長壽的蝴蝶及「囍」字，還有織錦圖畫，鈎針編織花紋，白帆布上配紅線十字繡等。

many children. There was also a superstition which held that the carrier must never be used the wrong side out, unless one parent was dead, and then it must be worn that way.

It was the custom for the grandmother to provide the carrier when the child was one month old. In the past they were made by hand by the donor, or else purchased from an embroiderer. Nowadays in Hong Kong, the women of the Tanka and Hoklo fishing communities still make their own carriers, but the Punti, or local Cantonese, and Hakka landdwellers and farmers buy theirs from market stalls.

## Cantonese and Hakka style

There were three main types of carrier. The first, and used by these two ethnic groups in Hong Kong, has a decorated centre square with straps which are a continuation of the top and bottom edges. Earlier carriers, dating back to the last century, were much larger than the ones of today, being 50-60cm square with straps extending to 110cm. At the end of one or both lower straps, the corners would be folded over to the centre to form a pocket in which to carry coins. The carriers were made of cotton or hemp, dyed purple/black or indigo blue, with the centres of embroidered silk or occasionally wool, or else left plain. Modern versions of this style are smaller and simpler in construction, and usually made of red or patterned cotton with an embroidered centre square. However, those made for presentation on a special occasion would be made of red satin or brocade.

The designs on the centres of the carriers were

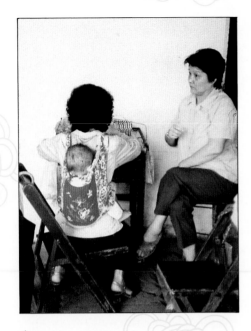

## 蜑家及鶴佬式

第二類背兒帶，多爲蜑家及鶴佬人使用，常見於漁村中。這類背兒帶的正方形部份較第一類爲小，布條則較長及交叉牢牢的縫於正方形的四角。

蜑家及鶴佬婦女鮮有在背兒帶上刺繡，相反，他們會在背兒帶的正方形布幅上釘上許多彩色棉布的三角形。布幅上方延伸出去的布條也佈滿裝飾，在使用時，人們可欣賞到布條上的華麗裝飾，與上世紀流行的「百家衣」相似。

手造之背兒帶通常是蜑家或鶴佬婦女在船上開暇時縫製。鶴佬婦女在縫造那些在特別日子及慶典時才使用的背兒帶時，往往會加上些鈴，除了作爲裝飾外，並可以驅走邪魔，還會用色彩繽紛的縫、膠珠等作爲裝飾。

△
廣東式背兒帶，新會，廣東，一九八七年。

Cantonese baby carrier. Xin Hui,
southern Guangdong, 1987.
(Copyright: V.M. Garrett)

▷
蜑家式背兒帶，嬰兒戴上銀腳鐲，澳門，一九八六年。

Tanka baby carrier; child wears silver anklet.
Macau, 1986.
(Copyright: V.V. Taylor)

a plethora of good luck symbols. The most common ones depicted were usually a combination of the following: a pair of mandarin ducks symbolizing marital fidelity; pomegranates for abundance in all things, especially children; lotus flowers which represent purity and fruitfulness; butterflies for conjugal happiness and long life; and the Chinese characters for double happiness, long life and good fortune. As well as embroidered cotton or silk, the centres were also made in many other ways, such as brocade pictures, crochet pictures, white canvas squares with red cross stitch, and interwoven strips of cotton.

## Tanka and Hoklo styles

A second shape favoured by the Tanka and Hoklo fishing people, and thus seen more often in the fishing villages, has a slightly smaller centre with longer straps fixed diagonally to the four corners of the square and much reinforcing stitching at these points.

The centres on carriers made by the Hoklo and Tanka women do not usually feature embroidery, but instead are made up of many coloured strips and triangles of cotton. These are appliqued onto the centre square, and continue up the top straps so that when worn the decoration is visible as far as the knot, reminiscient of the "Hundred Family Coats" of the last century. Hand sewn baby carriers are worked on whenever the woman has some free time on the junk, between cooking a meal, or helping the family to fish. Special ones made by the Hoklo women for festivals and celebrations have bells to frighten the bad spirits away, tassels, fringing, beading and applique in all the colours of the rainbow.

## 承托頭部之布幅

某些背兒帶的頂部會連着一幅布，以承托嬰兒頭部。有些是由棉布條縫成正方形格子，有些僅是一幅淨色布（蜑家婦女常用），其作用是托着嬰兒的頭及避免陽光照射。

## 樸素式

第三類背兒帶設計最簡單。只是一幅三米長，三十厘米闊的長方形紅色棉質或麻質布。傳統上，新郎在結婚時身上必掛紅。在科舉試高中的也掛紅。在婚禮後，紅布會暫時收起，以待日後之用。用法是用紅布把嬰兒包裹兩週，然後把嬰兒背上，在胸前打結。現在已很少人會用這類背兒帶了。

▷
水上人家之婦女使用未經修飾之紅棉質背兒帶背嬰兒，
大埔，香港，一九七九年。
Fisherwoman carrying child in plain undecorated red cotton baby carrier. Tai Po, Hong Kong, 1979.
(Garrett V.M., *Traditional Chinese Clothing in Hong Kong and South China*, Oxford University Press, 1987)

## Head Supports

Head supports were attached to the baby carriers. These were either made of strips of cotton stitched at intervals to form a lattice square, or were a rectangular piece of cloth (favoured especially by the Tanka women), and were attached to the top edge of the carrier to support the baby's head, and to shield it from the sun.

## Undecorated Style

The third style is the simplest of all, being a plain, undecorated strip of red cotton or hemp, approximately 3m long by 30cm wide. In the past it was a tradition for the bridegroom to wear a strip of red cloth draped across one shoulder of his long gown and tied on the opposite hip. (This red cloth had also been a feature of graduation dress for the successful candidates of the Imperial examinations, being tied diagonally across one shoulder for the first degree, and a second piece crossing from the other shoulder for the second degree.) After the wedding day it was then put aside for later use as a baby carrier, by winding the strip of cloth twice round the child, then tying in a knot in front of the wearer. It is seldom seen today although some fisherwomen use it as an alternative to the more elaborate styles.

## Baby Carrier Covers

Highly decorated baby carrier covers are made by the Hoklo women and are used on top of the baby carrier to protect the child when the weather is cold, as well as on special occasions. Embellished with embroidery, applique, braid, tassels and bells like the carriers, they are real works of art which take many months to

## 背兒帶蓋被

冬天天氣寒冷或在特別的日子，鶴佬婦女用背兒帶把嬰兒背上後，都愛再蓋上一塊背兒帶蓋被，既美觀，又可保暖。大部份背兒帶蓋被都是鶴佬婦女們的精心傑作，她們耗費長時間在蓋被上刺繡精細花紋及加上鈴、縫及編帶等作為裝飾，一如背兒帶那樣奪目。其他婦女則多使用款式簡單之背兒帶蓋被，如將兩塊已有圖案之棉布縫合起來，兩面都可使用。背兒帶蓋被亦是人們在農曆新年送贈的禮物、款式有紅色絲質、刺繡精細及有襯墊、有兜帽及夾毛等。

complete. Simpler covers were used by other ethnic groups, made of two layers of brightly patterned cotton stitched together so as to be reversible. The layers of cotton are pleated into a smaller band at the top, and two sets of ties held the cover in place around the child. Red silk ones, padded and embroidered, some with fur lining and hoods, were often given as gifts at Lunar New Year.

△
鶴佬婦女使用裝飾奪目之背兒帶蓋被蓋着嬰兒參加大皇爺誕，大埔、香港，一九七九年。

Hoklo woman carrying a child in a brightly decorated baby carrier cover while watching the Dai Wong Yeh festival at Tai Po, Hong Kong, 1979.
(Copyright: V.M. Garrett)

▷
一名婦人用繡上花紋之襯墊背兒帶蓋被抱着嬰兒。
西安，一九八三年。

Woman holding a child wrapped in an embroidered and padded baby carrier cover. Xian, 1983.
(Copyright: Niels Cross)

深藍和黑麻質背兒帶。中央之方格爲綠和粉紅色，並用齊針綉上孔雀、魚、花卉和壽字等圖案。廣東/客家，華南、十九世紀末。

Indigo and black dyed hemp baby carrier; callendered. Green and pink fine hemp panels; centre panel densely embroidered in satin and stem stitch, of peacocks, fish, flowers and *shou* character. Cantonese/Hakka South China, late 19thC.
50 cm H x 256 cm L

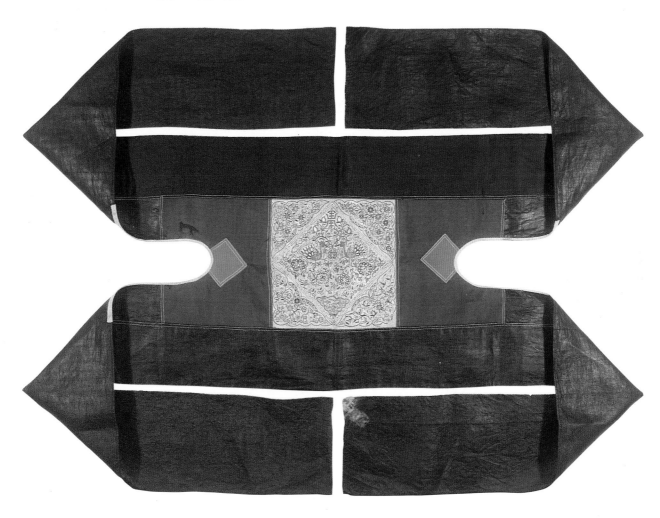

紅棉質背兒帶。中央爲織綿，繡上龍、鳳凰和"長命富貴"四個字。廣東/客家，元朗，一九七〇年代。

Red cotton baby carrier with silk brocade panel of four clawed dragon and phoenix and characters a wish for wealth and long life. Cantonese/Hakka, Yuen Long, 1970's.
40.5 cm H x 202 cm L

棉質貼布背兒帶，有珠子、編帶等裝飾。並加上紙板，增加堅挺程度。鶴佬，沙頭角，一九七〇年代。

Cotton patchwork and appliqued carrier with beads, ricrac and braid. Lined cardboard for stiffening. Hoklo, Shataukok, 1970's.
34 cm H x 200 cm L

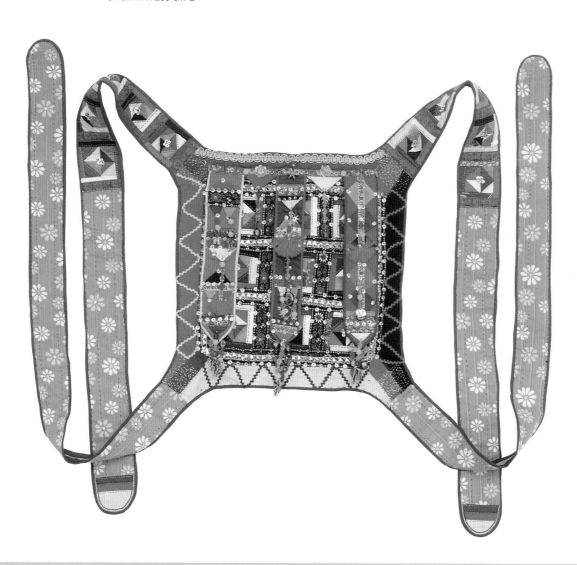

黑棉質背兒帶，用齊針繡上花藍、邊緣爲
典型之鶴佬式設計，並附有承托小孩頭部
之格子布網。鶴佬，廣東、約一九六〇年
代。

Black cotton carrier with satin stitch
embroidery of flower basket. Applique
design around edge is typical Hoklo
style. Lattice head support. Hoklo,
Guangdong, c. 1960's.
32 cm H x 204 cm L

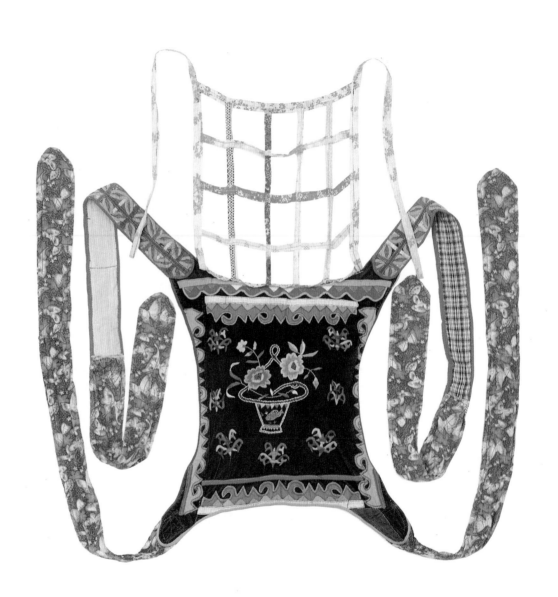

棉質印花布緄邊背兒帶，中央為"教堂窗花"紋樣貼布，並附有承托小孩頭部之格子布網。蜑家，廣東，約一九六〇年代。

Baby carrier with printed cotton edge
with "cathedral window" patchwork
centre. Lattice head support. Tanka,
Guangdong, c. 1960's.
34 cm H x 190 cm L

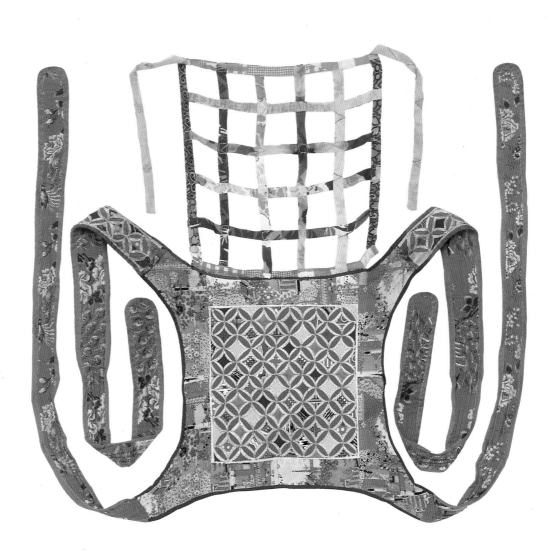

紅棉質印花背兒帶蓋被，花邊綑邊，並有
珠子和鈴作裝飾。鶴佬，沙頭角，
一九七〇年代。

Red printed cotton baby carrier cover
trimmed ricrac, braid beads, bells.
Hoklo, Shataukok, 1970's.
73 cm W x 74 cm H

黑棉質背兒帶蓋被，藍黃絅邊，有刺繡花
紋和金屬圓片裝飾。鶴佬，沙頭角，
約一九七〇年代。

Black cotton baby carrier cover with
blue and yellow edging. Trimmed ricrac,
embroidery and sequins, Hoklo,
Shataukok, c. 1970's.
70 cm W x 77 cm H

# 童 帽
# Children's Hats

在兒童的帽上加上吉祥圖案及護符的目的，是要嚇走鬼怪，由於女性一向不被重視，所以只有男童才會戴這些帽。

### 滿月帽
嬰兒滿月時，外祖母會造一頂紅色緞質或棉質的滿月帽給嬰兒。帽上之刺繡有花卉、水果及壽字，希望嬰兒長命及好運。

### 帽箍
帽箍是沒有頂部的帽，也是幼兒配戴的。帽箍的前幅多做成老虎、狗、豬等形狀，有些背面有尾巴。鶴佬兒童所戴的一種用黑棉布或黑膠紗所造，兩旁及前面中間有布造之花飾、邊緣用膠珠及花邊細邊，令整個帽箍看來耀眼非常。有些用鐵線將小動物及飾物繫於帽上，兒童走動時，這些飾物也隨而舞動。

### 狗頭帽
小孩在一歲後會戴黑或紅色的棉或緞質狗頭帽。帽的前幅會有部份反摺下來作爲耳朵，耳朵更會有軟毛，令形象更加神似。帽邊用不同顏色的棉布條細邊。有些狗頭帽上會縫上雀鳥及蝙蝠等裝飾，以幫助趕走魔鬼。總體來說，狗頭帽的保暖作用大於裝飾性。人們後來在帽的後面加上一塊小布幅，以保持兒童頸部溫暖。

Symbolism and charms were particularly noticeable on the elaborately decorated hats worn by all children until quite recently to scare away the evil spirits. During the last century when girls were considered to be of little importance, only boys would wear these hats. There were several types of hat a child could wear.

### First month cap
The first was worn from the age of one month, when it would be presented to the child, often by the maternal grandmother. Made from a strip of red satin or cotton gathered into a circle at the top with a centre back seam, it was frequently embroidered with designs of flowers, fruit, and the Chinese character *shou* to wish the child long life and good fortune.

### Open crown cap
The second type, also worn in infancy, was similar to the first, but the top of the crown was completely open. It often took the form of an animal such as a tiger, dog or pig, with a face at the front and sometimes with a padded tail at the back. Another style worn by Hoklo children comprised of a strip of cotton or *hak gow sa* (black gummed silk) joined at the back and

▷
頭戴滿月帽之小孩，十九世紀末。
Child wearing first month cap, late 19th century.
(Headland I.T., *Chinese Mother Goose Rhymes*, pub. 1900)

## 風帽

另一種冬天常戴的是風帽。風帽的外形與狗頭帽相似，不同的是在帽後的小布幅並不是加上去的，而是連着帽身的。大部份都加上墊裡，帽上繡雀鳥花卉圖案或獸面。帽的兩旁有繩圈，用來穿帶固定在頭部，帽後亦多有飄帶，飄帶尾還繫鈴作爲裝飾。

還有一種風帽有假耳朵的，在前額帽邊處加有繡花帶。鶴佬兒童仍戴這種風帽，以黑色棉布縫造，繡上飛機、船艇、昆蟲及雀鳥等圖案。

四邑兒童所戴的風帽以四十五厘米正方形紅色布對摺，頂部向下摺形成冠，兩角剪去，邊緣飾以編帶，並加上耳朵及背後的飄帶。

slightly gathered along the top edge. Above the ears and at the front were pleated fabric rosettes, and braid and beads decorated the edges. The whole effect was very colourful, some hats even having little animals and charms on wire which danced when the child moved.

## Dog head cap

When the child was about a year old it would wear the Dog's Head cap. This was made of black or red cotton or satin, with a seam running from centre front to centre back. A horizontal cut about a third of the way up from the front was folded down to give the impression of dog's ears. The edges were bound with contrast cotton, and the ears would sometimes have little tufts of fur to further suggest the animal. Some hats had decoration in the form of embroidered and appliqued birds and bats: additional help for the dog in his fight against evil. On the whole, however, this was a plain style which was worn more for warmth than decoration.

A further development was the Dog's Head cap with a back flap added, the purpose of which was to cover the back of the neck in cold weather. The crown was made separately from the brim, with the cut all the way round the head.

## Wind hat

Another style of cap for wearing in the winter was the Wind Hat. Shaped like the Dog's Head hat or with the crown gathered into a circle like a skull cap, the back flap was part of the hat and not an additional piece. This type was often lined and padded, some being embroidered with flowers and birds, while others had a fierce

animal face. Loops at the sides held tapes to
hold it under the chin, and long streamers hung
down the back with bells at the ends.

Another variation of the Wind Hat had imitation
ear flaps caught up and tied back with long
streamers, and an embroidered band placed
along the brim at the front. Hoklo children still
wear this style, made of black cotton with
modern embroidered designs of planes and
junks, as well as insects and birds.

A type worn by children from the area in the
Pearl River Delta known as *Sze Yap* was made
of a 45cm square of red cloth, placed on the
diagonal with the top corner folded down to
form the crown. The point was cut off and
sometimes ears were added. The edges were
trimmed with braid, and streamers at the back
held it close to the head.

## 虎頭帽

華北地區最流行的兒童帽爲虎頭帽，帽的外形一
望而知是老虎，雖然製造者可能未見過真的老
虎，但他會加上自己的想像力。大部份虎頭帽都
用橙色緞地黑色花紋，眼睛大而突出，口部張開
露出牙齒，尾巴加墊豎起。有些虎頭帽前部或其
上另繫一小虎，倍形威猛。

## 士人帽

隨着男童年紀漸長，所戴的帽已不再着重抵抗邪
魔，轉而着眼於他們的將來。因而給男孩子戴一
種士人帽，希望他們長大後能夠考取功名，爲家
族帶來名譽與財富。士人帽多爲黑色緞質，帽上
繡蝙蝠、花卉及宗教圖案。帽後多有兩條飄帶及
兩根羽毛狀帽飾。

## Tiger hat

The next style was the Tiger hat worn mostly
by children in northern China. There was no
mistaking what this style was meant to
represent: it came as close to being a tiger as the
maker could produce, usually without having
seen one, which made for some strange
interpretations! Most hats were made with an
orange satin crown marked with black stripes or
"eyes", and with ears, large protruding eyes, a
mouth full of bared teeth, and a padded tail
standing up at the back. Some versions had
another tiger suspended from wire at the front,
or on top of the hat, to give greater protection.

## Scholar hat

As the boy grew older, hats were worn less to

## 瓜皮帽

男孩子戴的一種帽爲瓜皮帽，黑色緞質素面無紋飾。帽身分爲六瓣，有摺邊。帽頂用黑色鈕或紅色毛球固定帽形。後期的瓜皮帽背後加上假辮，以代表滿清入主中原統治漢族後，強迫漢人男子要留的髮式。雖然在滿清被推翻後，此規定已廢除，但這種帽子依然爲人們所佩帶。在農曆新年，男孩子如穿上長衫馬褂，都愛戴這種瓜皮帽，以示隆重。

▷

男童穿着長衫、背心，頭戴瓜皮帽。農曆新年，一九八六年。

Little boy wearing *cheung sam,* waistcoat and skull cap; Lunar New Year, 1986.
(South China Morning Post)

guard against evil, and more to bring success for the future. A plainer style of hat known as the Scholar cap was given to a boy child in the hope that he would do well in the official examinations, and thus bring wealth and distinction to his clan. Made of black satin, it was embroidered with bats, flowers and religious symbols. At the back were often two streamers and two pointed "feathers".

## Skull cap

For everyday wear boys wore the plain black satin skull cap. It was made from six segments fixed to a narrow brim, stiffened and topped with a black button or red pompom. Some later hats had a false queue of hair attached to represent the hairstyle imposed upon the conquered Chinese males by the ruling Manchu government. This Manchu custom was outlawed at the overthrow of the Qing dynasty, but by that time it had become desirable and respectable. Now considered formal wear, the skull cap is still seen occasionally at the Lunar New Year if the boy is dressed in his *cheung sam ma kua.*

## Crown

For festival wear, a style more like a crown than a hat was worn by children up to the age of six or seven at important occasions such as the Lunar New Year. Today, the crown is worn by the Hoklo children at major celebrations. It was made of stiffened card covered with fabric and decorated with embroidery, sequins and braid, with streamers hanging down the back. Tassels hung from the sides, and silk puff balls and stuffed toy animals and birds were attached to wire springs to make them dance when the child moved.

81

## 冠

在節日裏，六、七歲以下的兒童多戴冠，尤其是農曆新年。現在則只有鶴佬兒童在重要的慶典中才戴冠。冠是在硬紙上加上布，再繡上花紋圖案，及加上金屬片、膠珠等裝飾。冠後面則有飄帶，兩旁有縫和絲絨球。有些更用彈簧將毛製動物和雀鳥附於冠上，當兒童行走時，它們也一同舞動。

## 假辮帽

這類帽的邊緣及背後連着的一條假辮用黑色絲線造成。帽身通常分為八瓣，每瓣都繡上圖案，常見的有八仙像。

## False queue

A final style is the hat with a false fringe and queue made of black twisted silk thread. The crown is divided into eight sections, each embroidered, often with the emblems of the Eight Immortals.

兩名小童戴着冠、口圍和鎖。農曆新年，一九〇九年。
Two children wearing crowns, collar and padlock;
Lunar New Year, 1909.
(Public Records Office)

紅色印花棉質狗頭帽，兩邊近耳朵處有軟毛，棉布條綑邊。東莞，廣東，約一九五〇年代。 ▷

Printed cotton Dog Head cap with fur at 'ears', bound cotton at edges. Dongguan, Guangdong, c. 1950's.
15 cm Dia.

◁ 紅黑棉質帽箍，有大量金屬圓片、刺繡花紋、緣、及襯墊蝴蝶、雀鳥等作裝飾。鶴佬，沙頭角，香港，約一九七〇年代。

Black and red cotton hat, open crown style, heavily decorated with sequins, embroidery, tassels and padded butterflies and birds. Hoklo, Shataukok, Hong Kong, c. 1970's.
16 cm Dia.

橙色帽箍,額前爲老虎樣子,有鬚及尾 ▷
巴。華北,二十世紀初。

Headband with tiger face at front,
appliqued and embroidered, tassels
and padded tail; north China, early
20thC.
12 cm Dia.

◁ 橙緞質虎頭帽,黑色花紋,耳朶內有白兔
公仔,並有襯墊尾巴。華北,十九世紀
末。

Orange satin tiger hat with black
embroidered 'stripes'. Rabbits in ears,
padded tail. North China, late 19thC.
15 cm Dia.

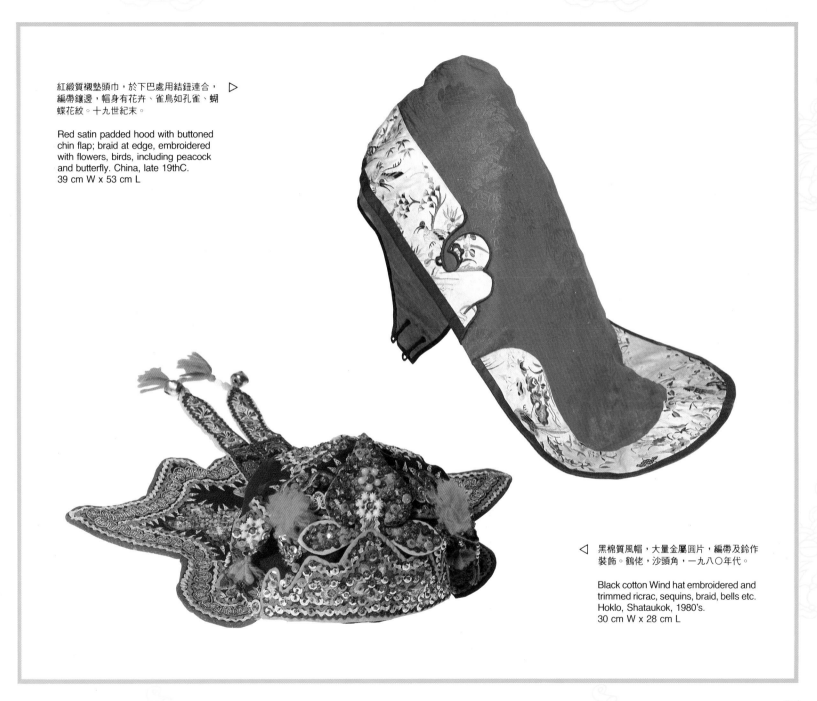

紅緞質襯墊頭巾，於下巴處用結鈕連合，編帶鑲邊，帽身有花卉、雀鳥如孔雀、蝴蝶花紋。十九世紀末。 ▷

Red satin padded hood with buttoned chin flap; braid at edge, embroidered with flowers, birds, including peacock and butterfly. China, late 19thC.
39 cm W x 53 cm L

◁ 黑棉質風帽，大量金屬圓片，編帶及鈴作裝飾。鶴佬，沙頭角，一九八〇年代。

Black cotton Wind hat embroidered and trimmed ricrac, sequins, braid, bells etc. Hoklo, Shataukok, 1980's.
30 cm W x 28 cm L

藍緞質冠。冠分爲兩部份，一部份用北京
結組成「壽」字和繡上花卉，另一部份用
齊針繡上花卉。十九世紀末。 ▷

Blue satin crown with Peking knot
embroidery of *shou* character and
flowers on one side, and satin stitch
embroidery of flowers on other side.
China, late 19thC.
15 cm Dia.

黑藍緞質士人帽，用鎖繡針法繡上雲之花 ▽
紋和打結。帽後有飄帶。華北，十九世紀
末。

Black and blue satin Scholar's hat with
chain stitch embroidery of endless knot,
clouds, streamers at back. North China,
late 19thC.
14 cm Dia.

86

黑緞質男童瓜皮帽，帽身分爲六瓣及有反 ▷
邊。頂部有深紅色絨球。多在農曆新年時
戴。香港，二十世紀中葉。

Boy's back satin skull cap, 6 segments
and brim; dark red pompom; worn at
Lunar New Year. Hong Kong, mid 20thC.
15 cm Dia.

◁  黑棉質狗頭帽，用鎮繡針法繡上雀鳥和蝴
蝶花紋。兩旁有鈴作裝飾。鶴佬，廣東，
一九六〇年代。

Black cotton Dog Head cap
embroidered chain stitch birds and
butterfly; ricrac, bells at sides; Hoklo,
Guangdong, c. 1960's.
14 cm Dia.

黑緞質假辮帽，帽身分為八瓣，繡上八
仙，並有一小孩在中央。正面有假邊及
縧，帽後有假辮。華北，十九世紀。

Black satin hat with crown of 8 segments
each embroidered with the emblems of
the Eight Immortals, with padded figure
of baby in centre, tassels, false fringe at
front, and false queue at back. North
China, 19thC.
16 cm Dia.

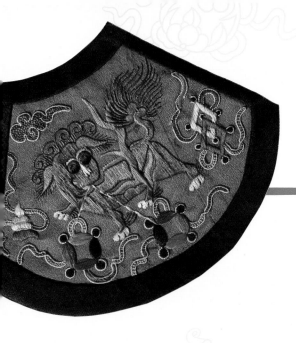

# 佩飾
# Accessories

## 口圍

口圍是幼兒佩帶的，有刺繡紋的口圍通常由數瓣組成，一般五瓣，有些再細分爲數瓣，每一瓣都繡上吉祥圖案，現仍可見。

有些口圍是做成猛獸形狀的，常見有老虎或狗，藉以保護兒童。

香港的鶴佬兒童，在六、七歲前遇到特別的日子或節日，都會戴一些特別的口圍，口圍由一塊環狀的棉布縫成，繡滿各種顏色的棉縫飾綑邊，珠及金屬片，口圍邊釘上用珠子造成的縫。這些口圍多由母親所做。

## 耳套

耳套是較年長的女童的恩物。耳套成心形內有墊裡，在冬天用來套着雙耳保暖。耳套的邊緣多有軟毛作爲裝飾，套面亦會繡上花卉及雀鳥等圖案。

## 童鞋
### 長筒靴

用背兒帶背着的幼兒多穿紅、橙和紫等顏色十分鮮艷的緞質長筒靴。靴上繡滿各種圖案，例如代表皇帝之龍、代表皇后之鳳、代表有餘之魚、代表步步高陞之鹿等。除此之外，還有用鐵線將小

## Collars

Collars were worn by very young children. Embroidered ones were made of several segments, usually five, while some were elaborately subdivided into many smaller sections, and each segment was decorated with auspicious symbols. Five segment collars are still seen today, made of plain and printed cottons.

Collars shaped like a fierce animal's body, often the tiger or dog were common. The animal appeared to be coiled round the child's neck to give greater protection.

The Hoklo children in Hong Kong wear very elaborate collars on special occasions and festivals. The collars are made of a circular piece of cotton with a back opening, and decorated with beads, sequins, braid, coloured cotton applique and beaded tassels hanging all round the edge. These are made by the mother or bought from an embroiderer living locally, and worn by the child up to the age of six or seven.

## Earmuffs

Ear muffs were an accessory worn by older

型襯墊動物或雀鳥縛在鞋頭或在鞋頭釘上五彩縫及毛球。

### 動物鞋

和童帽一樣，童鞋也多成狗、貓、虎和豬等動物形狀，驅嚇鬼怪，有些更在鞋釘上鈴。童鞋多是棉質和緞質的，鞋面繡滿顏色鮮艷的花紋，鞋底加上棉墊。

### 纏足鞋

女孩子到了三歲至五歲期間，便需要纏足。大約在九、十世紀，朝廷的婦女開始纏足後，這習俗便在整個中國流行起來。除了滿族、客家婦女和需要下田或居於水上的貧窮的婦女外，其他婦女都需要纏足。少女由三、四歲開始纏足，直至她長大成人，她的腳掌大約只有五吋長，三吋金蓮是極少有的，這種人必須是不需要做任何家務或工作，走路時還須有僕人參扶。

隨着十九世紀末西方思想的傳入，纏足這習俗已開始式微。不少反對纏足的團體紛紛成立，鼓吹拼棄這個惡習，一九一二年，隨着中華民國的成立，纏足始被廢除。

### 男童鞋

年紀較長的男童所穿着的多是黑色緞質，白色厚底鞋，和成年男性穿的十分相似，但鞋的顏色較爲鮮艷，並繡上吉祥花卉及昆蟲。鞋面中央部位有一條縫，上以皮革加固，伸延至鞋的底部，使走路時鞋底更有彈性。鞋底有一層皮革，皮革上面再加一層厚而漿過的紙，邊緣漂白。據説這些紙張不少來自上世紀傳教士所派發的聖經。

girls. Padded and lined, and shaped like a heart, they slipped over the ears to keep them warm in cold weather and had tapes which tied under the chin. They were often trimmed with fur at the edges to represent an animal and embroidered with flowers and birds.

## Children's Footwear

### Bootees

Very young children would wear satin bootees when carried in their baby carrier on special occasions. Viewed from the front these were most colourful, made of red, orange or purple satin embroidered with designs of the dragon, the symbol of the Emperor, or the phoenix, an ancient figure signifying goodness and benevolence and the symbol of the Empress. Fish, symbol of abundance in all things, and deer, symbol of advancement and good fortune were also used. Often padded animals and birds were suspended above the toe on wires and long coloured tassels hung from the front, together with multi-coloured bobbles. Some styles also had a false shoe fixed to the bottom for a slightly older baby.

### Animal shoes

Like the hats, children's footwear was also made in the form of a dog, cat, tiger, or pig for the purpose of frightening away bad spirits. Large eyes to see evil lurking, large furry ears to hear it, and whiskers, all helped to suggest the creature being represented. Usually made of red cotton or satin, with brightly embroidered uppers and padded cotton soles, some shoes even had bells on the toes to produce an audible warning for the spirits.

中國男孩樣子的玩具公仔，身體用棉花造，頭和手則爲紙板造。身穿緞質刺繡衫和褲；頭戴有釘上護符和錢幣的棉質帽。這種玩具一般作出口用途。十九世紀。

Chinese boy doll with cotton stuffed body and papier mache head and hands. Dressed in embroidered satin *sam* and trousers; cotton cap with amulets and coin on cord.
Possibly made for export, China, 19th C.

## Bound feet shoes

When a girl was aged between three and five years, she would begin to bind her feet. The fashion, which had begun in the ninth or tenth century among the women at court, was almost universal throughout China, with the exception of Manchu women, the Hakka women and the poorest women who worked in the fields or lived on the water. A binding cloth of finely woven cotton or silk, about 2m long, was wrapped around the foot, starting at the toes which were pressed back into the instep, and finishing at the heel. When the girl was fully grown, her feet were usually bound to a length of 12 cm: the 8 cm lotus was quite rare, and only for those women who did no work, and had servants to support them while walking.

Due to western influences at the end of the 19th century, the fashion began to decline. Various anti-footbinding societies were formed to promote its demise: it was banned by the new Republic in 1912, and finally died out in the 1930's.

## Older boys

Shoes for older boys were made of black satin with a thick white sole, similar to those worn by the men, albeit more colourful. The sole consisted of a layer of thin leather above which was a thick layer of pasted paper whitened around the edges, some said to be cut from the numerous Bibles distributed by the missionaries during the last century! The uppers were sometimes embroidered with auspicious flowers and insects, and with a centre seam reinforced with leather, extended over the rigid sole to give sufficient spring for walking.

多瓣絲質口圍，繡上動物和花卉圖案，正面有三隻眼睛，十九世紀。

Silk collar with many segments, embroidered animals and flowers. Three eyes at front. China, 19thC. 27 cm Dia.

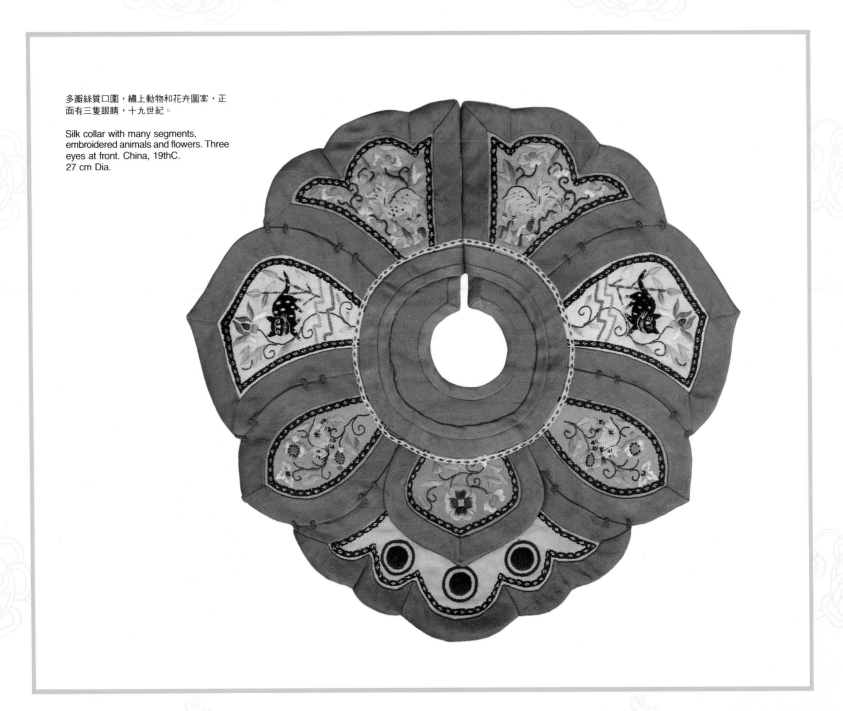

92

五瓣緞質口圍，每瓣都繡上不同之動物，包括貓、獅子、鹿、豬及老虎。還有五毒，蓮花等。十九世紀。

Satin collar in five segments. Different animal in each: cat, lion, deer, pig, tiger. Also Five Poisons, lotus flowers, endless knot etc. China, 19thC.
23 cm Dia.

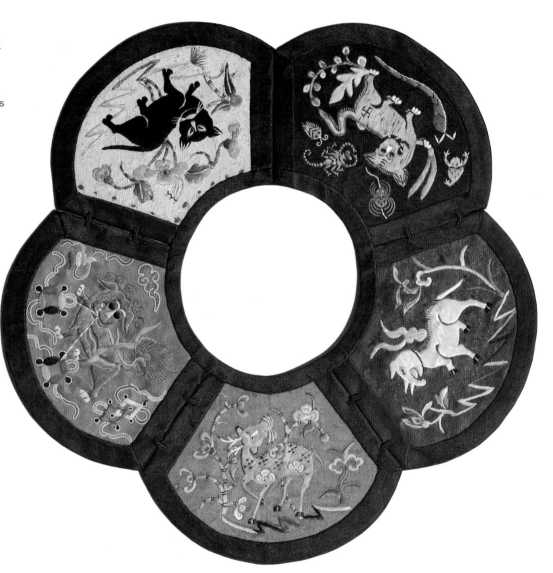

橙緞質虎形口圍，有大眼睛、耳朵、鼻子和口。中央有一"王"字。華北，十九世紀。

Orange satin tiger collar with large ears, eyes, nose and mouth: Centre character stands for "prince". N. China, 19thC. 30 cm Dia.

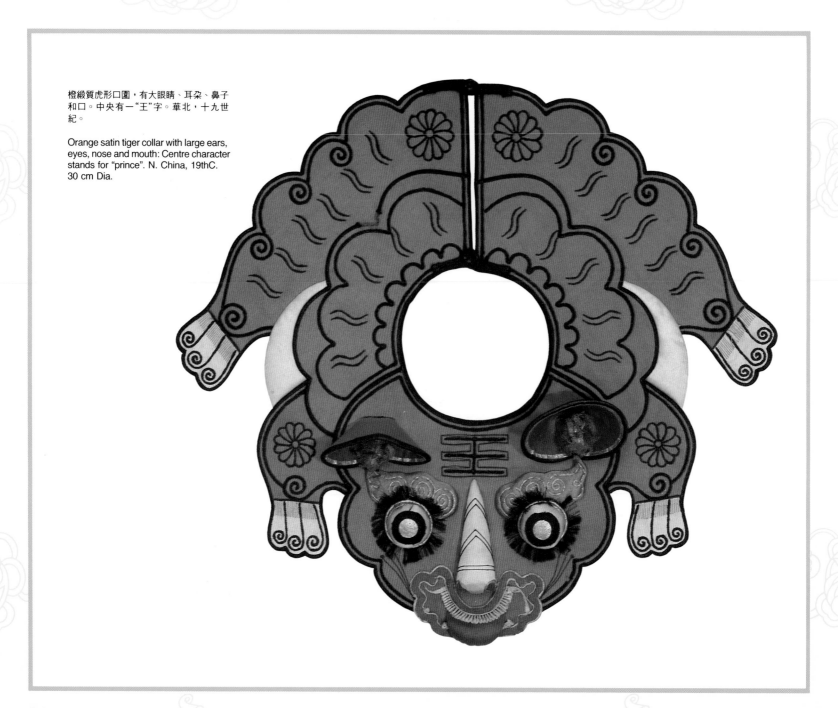

藍緞質耳套，繡上在花叢中的鹿，並腳踏 ▷
靈芝。十九世紀。

Blue satin ear muffs embroidered deer
amid flowers, walking over sacred
fungus. China, 19thC.
9 cm W x 11 cm H

◁ 藍絲質耳套，中央爲黃色結和蝴蝶圖案。
邊緣有軟毛。兩個耳套用黑布條連着。十
九世紀。

Blue silk ear muffs with yellow centres.
Embroidery of endless knot, butterflies
etc. Trimmed fur at outer edges. Black
cotton satin ties. China, 19thC.
9.5 cm W x 10.5 cm H

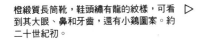

橙緞質長筒靴，鞋頭繡有龍的紋樣，可看 ▷
到其大眼、鼻和牙齒，還有小雞圖案。約
二十世紀初。

Orange satin bootees. Dragons
embroidered with large eyes, nose and
teeth at toes, with cockerel novering
above. China, c. early 20thC.
10 cm L x 15 cm H

◁ 紅棉質豬頭鞋，西安，一九六〇年代。

Red cotton shoes embroidered to
represent pig. Xian, 1960's.
15 cm L

96

紅緞質魚鞋，鞋身釘上金屬圓片代表魚 ▷
鱗。昆明，一九八○年代。

Red satin fish shoes with embroidery
and sequins to represent scales.
Kunming, 1980's.
12 cm L

◁ 褐紅棉質貓頭鞋，鞋頭有彩色刺繡，棉質
鞋底。西安，一九八○年代。

Maroon cotton cat shoes with multi
coloured embroidery on toes and cotton
soles. Xian, 1980's.
13 cm L

紅緞質動物鞋，樣子兇惡，綠色耳朵，黃色羽毛，白棉質鞋底。華北，二十世紀中葉。 ▷

Fierce animal shoes of red satin, with green satin ears, yellow fur. White cotton stitched soles.
Northern China, mid 20thC.
15 cm L

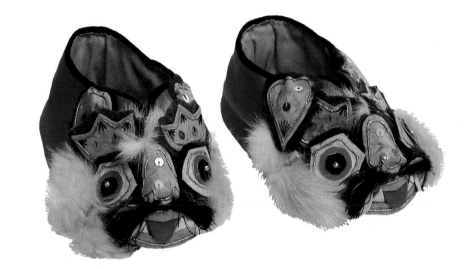

◁ 紅緞質童鞋，鞋頭繡上蟹的紋樣，鞋邊繡上五毒圖案，鞋的內部則貼上石榴紙樣。一九三〇年代。

Red satin shoes embroidered with green crabs on toes. Four of the Five Poisons embroidered at sides. Paper pomegrenate pasted onto inside soles.
China, c. 1930's.
15 cm L

粉紅緞質纏足鞋，鞋身用金線及齊針繡上
花紋。鞋跟有圖案棉墊。並附有一個曾經
被福建省浸信會傳道會使用過之石膏腳模
型。十九世紀。

Pink satin shoe with embroidery of satin
stitch and couched gold thread.
Patterned cotton heel support. Plaster
foot mould used by Baptist Missionary
Society in Fujian province. 19thC.
8 cm x 11 cm H

黑絨布男童鞋，鞋頭有一條綠色皮革。白 ▷
棉質襯墊鞋底。華北，十九世紀。

Boys' black velvet embroidered shoes
with green leather strip at toes. Stitched
white cotton soles, and padded uppers.
Northern China, 19thC.
18 cm L

◁ 草鞋，鞋底近鞋頭處加入黑和藍棉布條織
成。華南，十九世紀。

Woven straw shoes, uppers and soles
both of straw. Strips of black and blue
cotton woven across soles near toes.
South China, 19thC.
15 cm L

# 飾 物 與 護 符
# Jewellery and Charms

護符在兒童的衣服上佔有相當重要地位，其主要用途在於保護兒童，抵抗鬼怪。護符飾物有銀、"白銅"、黃銅及鍍銀的，多是家庭成員或親友在兒童滿月時送給兒童的，此習俗現仍流行。

## 綴在帽上之護符

用銀或銅造之護符通常會釘在帽的前幅。最常用的人物有八仙和壽星。人們認爲八仙及壽星皆爲王母娘娘祝壽而來，代表長壽快樂。佛像亦是人們常用的。一個或一排多個笑佛也是釘在帽的前幅，人們相信佛佗能解除人世間之憂困。

除此之外，還有一些寓意吉祥的護符，如八卦是周易中的八種基本圖形。八卦是由八組斷續不一的線所組成的圓圈，中央爲一個陰陽符號。

## 鈴

在嬰兒滿月時，父母通常都會給嬰兒掛上鈴作爲護符，其用意是利用鈴所發出之聲響嚇走鬼怪，水上居民尤其喜愛。他們多將鈴繫於腳鐲或用紅線將鈴繫於腳上。用來縛緊帽之繩子也常飾以鈴。

Lucky charms for protection against evil were an important part of children's dress. Silver, *pak tong* (white brass), gilded silver or brass jewellery was given to the child by family members and friends, usually at the first month celebration. This is still the custom in many parts of China.

## Amulets used on Hats

Amulets stamped out of a thin sheet of silver or brass were often stitched across the front of the hat. The most popular were the Eight Immortals worn with the God of Longevity, Shou Hsing, in the centre. These were normally shown together because the Eight Immortals and Shou Hsing were said to be guests of the Queen at the latter's annual birthday feast in the Western Heavens. A single or row of Laughing Buddhas were also placed across the front of the cap. He is a friendly figure said to be able dismiss misery and unhappiness from the world.

Other amulets depicted Chinese characters for good luck and long life, but one which was frequently worn on hats to ensure continued good fortune was the Pak Kwa, also known as Eight Trigrams and the basis of an ancient system of divination and philosophy. This was

▷

小童腳戴銀鍊和鈴，手纏紅線和戴玉手鐲，東涌，
大嶼山，香港，一九七九年。

Child wearing silver chain and bells round ankle; red
thread and a jade bangle on the wrist. Tung Chung,
Lantau Island, Hong Kong, 1979.
(Copyright: V.M. Garrett)

a mystical symbol showing eight groups of
broken and unbroken lines arranged in a circle
sometimes with the *yin yang* symbol of creation
in the centre.

## Bells
Bells to scare off bad spirits with their noise
were part of the charms given to the baby at the
first month celebration. Two anklets with bells
on them, or a large single brass bell tied to the
ankle with red string were especially popular
with the fishing people's children. Bells were
also attached to the cap strings at the back of the
hats.

## Charms worn round the Neck
The God of Longevity was also worn as a charm
around the child's neck, where he is shown
either mounted or standing beside a deer or
*ch'i-lin* holding a peach for immortality in one
hand and a staff in the other. The *ch'i-lin* is
often used as an auspicious symbol for children
and is a mythical beast with a dragon's head,
one or more horns, a scaly body and a bushy
lion's tail. It is thought to have great wisdom,
and is a desire for a large family of sons who do
well in the Imperial examinations.

A very common tradition was the wearing of a
silver padlock, inscribed with propitious
characters and symbols, around the neck to
"lock the child to earth". These are seldom seen
nowadays, however the Hoklo children still
wear an enamelled *pak tong* padlock in the shape
of a butterfly, symbol of happiness and long
life. Padlocks were sometimes attached to a
chain, or else joined to a large metal ring which
was large enough to go over the child's head.
This metal ring was also used alone: meant to be

### 頸部之護符
人們喜歡佩帶「壽星」飾牌於頸上。其造型多是
騎在麒麟或鹿之上或站於其旁邊，一隻手捧着蟠
桃，另一隻手拄着一枝杖。對於兒童來說，麒麟
是吉祥之物，麒麟乃神話裏的動物，龍頭、獅子
尾，有角，全身滿佈鱗片，被喻爲充滿智慧，象
徵多子登科。

佩帶吉祥圖案或字句之銀鎖也非常普遍，其用意
是保護兒童之生命。現在已較少人佩帶，但仍有
很多鶴佬人佩帶蝴蝶形 " 白銅 " 鎖，寓意快樂長

壽。人們多將銀鎖用鍊或金屬圈串起來佩帶，有時候亦會單獨佩帶金屬圈，目的是要使鬼怪誤以爲小童衹是動物，不傷害他們。佩帶金或玉造之佛像吊墜或銀造之桃形吊墜之習慣至今不衰。

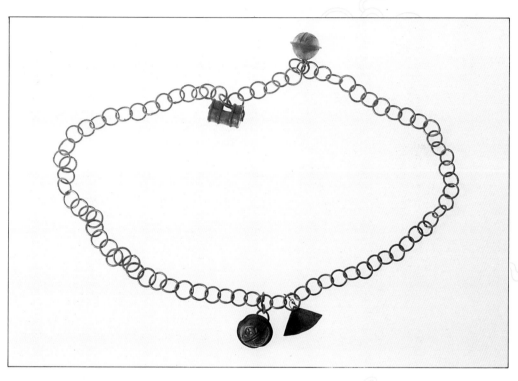

銀頸鍊連鎖、兩個鈴和三角形飾物。蜑家，珠江三角州，二十世紀中葉。

Silver chain necklace with padlock, 2 bells and triangle. *Sui-seung* people, Pearl River delta, mid 20th C.
23cm Dia.

## 錢幣

錢幣代表了財富，加上人們認爲歷代皇朝之錢幣具有保護佩帶者的力量，錢幣又是財富象徵，因此將錢幣作爲兒童飾物的一種。人們用紅線將錢幣串起掛於兒童頸上，亦有縛在帽繩之上。

## 紙造之護符

水上居民多佩帶紙造之護符。人們把護符咒寫在黃色的紙上，再將黃色紙用紅布包着，然後釘在兒童的衣服上，又或者用線或金屬圈圍於頸上。

the equivalent of a dog collar, it was thought to fool the evil spirits into thinking the child was an animal, and therefore of no value.

Other charms of silver or carved peach stone kernels were worn in the form of a necklace, and pendants of gold or jade buddhas are still popular today.

## Coins

Cash coins were used in many ways as a charm for children. Old coins from past dynasties were thought to have powers of protection, while the coin is always a symbol of wealth. They were hung on red cord around the child's neck, or else attached as a weight on the cap strings taken under the chin.

## Paper Charms

Paper charms were also worn and are still used today by the children of the fishing people. A charm was written on yellow paper then wrapped in red cloth and pinned to the child's clothing or suspended from a string or metal ring around the neck of the child who, in summer on the boat, might otherwise be completely naked.

## Thread

Red thread was also propitious and said to ensure long life. An old tradition was that after the birth of a baby, neighbours and friends would give pieces of thread which were then combined into a tassel and hung on the baby's clothes. This was called the "Hundred Families Tassel" and signified a wish for good fortune for the child from many families.

Another use of thread was discovered by the

## 線

紅線代表吉利和長壽。中國有一種習俗，當某戶有嬰兒出生，其鄰居或朋友會贈送一些紅線給嬰兒，其父母便將這些線縫合成縫，釘在嬰兒的衣服上，名爲「百家縫」，寓意各人都爲嬰兒作福。

在新界邊區木湖村，線有另一種用途。在嬰兒出生後，其母親會將兩枝針平放在一頂給嬰兒之帽的前幅，然後用紅色及綠色的線繞纏着，寓意長壽。

人們亦把紅線繫於手腕及腳腕處，或以之把玉鐲及腳鐲縛緊在手和腳上，以防鬆脱。

author in the village of Muk Wu in the border area of the New Territories. On the birth of a child, a mother put two pins horizontally on the front of the little embroidered cap worn from the age of one month. Round these pins were wound red and green thread as a wish for long life.

Red thread was often tied around the wrists or ankles of the child, sometimes also fastened to the jade bangle or silver anklet, presumably to stop it falling off inadvertantly.

紫緞質冠，冠後有粉紅色飄帶。冠身有毛球、鈴和用平金法繡上花卉圖案繡邊。冠的正面有壽星像，像下有一個八卦，並有"長命富貴"四個字。上海，二十世紀初。 ▷

Crown in purple satin, lined red cotton. Pink streamers at back. Puff balls and bells. Floss embroidery flowers edged silver couching. Four amulets at front with characters for wealth and long life. *Pa Kua* at centre front with Shou Hsing above it. Shanghai, early 20thC. 13 cm Dia.

◁ 紅緞質冠，有毛球和繸。帽的正面中央是壽星和八卦，兩旁有八仙。
上海，二十世紀初。

Red satin crown with puff balls and tassels. Eight Immortals across front, with *Pa Kua* and Shou Hsing at centre. Shanghai, early 20thC. 13 cm Dia.

藍絲質襯墊帽箍，於耳處有絲縫，帽的正
面有九個佛像，中間的一個較大。在佛像
之下有一排金屬飾鈕。十九世紀。

Open crown hat of blue silk, padded,
trimmed with fringing at 'ears'. Metal
studs across front and 8 small, and 1
large Buddha. China, 19thC.
16 cm Dia.

綠絲質襯墊風帽，粉紅和藍絲質編帶和黑
棉布鑲邊。帽後有飄帶，帽的前面中間有
壽星，兩旁有八仙，其下有一排金屬飾
鈕，帽後有"和合二仙"飾牌及五顆桃飾。
帽繩連着一個錢幣。十九世紀。

Wind hat of green silk, padded, lined
fleecy cotton. Edged pink/blue silk braid
and black cotton. Streamers at back.
Eight Immortals and Shou Hsing in
centre with metal studs at front. Amulet
with Heavenly Twins and 5 peach stones
at back. Coin on neck cord. 19thC.
32 cm L x 36 cm W.

琺瑯及"白銅"蝴蝶形鎖連鍊。鍊上連着一刀一劍、兩尾魚、兩個八卦及一顆桃飾。鶴佬、沙頭角，約一九六〇年。

Enamel and *pak tong* butterfly lock and chain, with 2 swords (male and female), 2 fish, 2 *pa kua* and a peach stone. Hoklo, Shataukok, c. 1960. 18 cm Dia.

銀鎖。一面有中國和俄國國旗及"和平"二字，另一面有「百家保」三個字。鎖下連着三顆桃形鐺鈴。約一九五〇年代。

Silver padlock with Chinese flag and Russian flag, and characters for peace and safety on one side, and characters on back calling for protection for many homes. 3 bells in the form of peach stones. China, c. 1950's. 5 cm W x 4 cm H

"白銅"項圈，吊墜為一男孩騎在麒麟上。▷
十九世紀末。

Neckring of metal *pak tong* with a boy
riding on a *chilin*. China, late 19thC.
17 cm Dia.

"白銅"項圈連鎖及四顆扁身桃飾。廣州，▷
十九世紀。

Neckring of *pak tong* with padlock and
four flat carved peach stones.
Guangzhou, 19thC.
13.5 cm Dia.

108

# 參考書目 Selected Bibliography

## 第一章　PART I

張紫晨:《中國民俗與民俗學》,浙江人民出版社,1985。

沈從文:《中國古代服飾研究》。商務印書館香港分館,1981。

杜書華:"古畫中的兒童天地",《故宮文物月刊》,1986,第四卷第一期,4-15頁。

劉芳如:"著色鮮潤、體度如生:蘇漢臣嬰戲圖試析",《故宮文物月刊》,1990,第八卷第一期,78-95頁。

畏冬:《中國古代兒童題材繪畫》,紫禁城出版社,1987。

中國美術全集編輯委員會:《中國美術全集工藝美術編》(12),人民美術出版社、上海人民美術出版社、文物出版社和中國建築工業出版社聯合出版,1988。

周汛、高明:《中國古代服飾風俗》,陝西人民出版社,1988。

張輔元:《商品史話》,遼寧人民出版社,1988。

俞松年、茅家義、毛大倫、劉文萱:《生活名物史話》,上海人民出版社,1988。

河南省博物館編:《河南省博物館》,文物出版社,1985。

王亞蓉:《中國民間刺繡》,商務印書館,1985。

古元:《民間藝術瑰寶》,陝西人民美術出版社,1988。

粘碧華:《刺繡首飾》,海風出版社有限公司,1987。

朱培初:《中國的刺繡》,人民出版社,1987。

江紹原:《髮鬚爪》,上海文藝出版社,1987。

丘桓興:《中國民俗採英錄》,湖南文藝出版社,1987。

謝克:《中國木版年畫》,香港大一出版部,1985。

姚元龍:《吉祥圖案資料》,上海書局出版社,1989。

藝術家雜誌主編:《中國鄉土藝術》,藝術家出版社,1987。

李霖燦:《中國風俗畫欣賞》,行政院文化建設委員會印行,1989。

施宣圓、王有爲、丁鳳麟、吳根梁主編:《中國文化辭典》,上海社會科學院,1987。

鄭傳寅、張健主編:《中國民俗辭典》,湖北辭書出版社,1987。

袁珂編著:《中國神話傳說詞典》,上海辭書出版社,1985。

中央工藝美術學院編著:《工藝美術辭典》,黑龍江人民出版社,1988。

夏元瑜:《金鼎夢》,九歌出版社,1985。

Chiang, Yee, *A Chinese Childhood*, London: Methuen & Co. Ltd., 1940.

Berliner, Nancy Zeng, *Chinese Folk Art*, Boston: Little, Brown and Company, 1986.

Fawdry, Marguerite, *Chinese Childhood*, London: Pollock's Toy Theatres Limited, 1977.

## 第二章 PART II

Burkhardt, V.R., *Chinese Creeds and Customs, Vols 1-3,* South China Morning Post, Hong Kong, 1955-9.

Ball, J. Dyer, *Things Chinese,* reprint, Oxford University Press, Hong Kong, 1982.

Doolittle, Rev. J., *Social life of the Chinese, Vols I and II,* New York, 1865.

Eberhard, Wolfram, *A Dictionary of Chinese Symbols,* Routledge & Kegan Paul, New York, 1986.

Garrett, Valery M., *Traditional Chinese Clothing in Hong Kong and South China, 1840-1980,* Oxford University Press, Hong Kong, 1987.

Goodrich, L. Carrington, *15th Century Illustrated Chinese Primer, Hsin-pien tui-hsiang szu-yen,* Hong Kong University Press, Hong Kong, 1975.

Levy, Howard S., *Chinese Footbinding,* Neville Spearman, London, 1966.

Williams, C.A.S., *Outlines of Chinese Symbolism and Art Motives,* Customs College Press, Peking, 1931.

# 鳴謝 Acknowledgements

本展覽及目錄於籌辦過程中，蒙下列熱心人士及機構鼎力協助，謹此申謝。

The Museum is deeply indebted to the following individuals and institutions for their assistance and support in producing the "Children of the Gods – Dress and Symbolism in China" exhibition and the publication of this catalogue.

鍾燕齊先生

符俊強先生

黎玉英女士

施天賜博士

蘇崇尹先生

謝克先生

余詠宇女士

楊廣顯先生

杜麗莎高文女士

馮守仁先生

賈納先生

許舒博士

苗力知先生

蔡淑華女士

尹若蓮女士

河南省博物館

市政局香港藝術館

香港旅遊協會

牛津大學出版社

香港政府檔案處

區域市政局三棟屋博物館

東涌官立小學

Mr. Joel Chung

Mr. Stanley Fu

Ms. Yuk-ying Lai

Dr. Janet Lee Scott

Mr. Sung-wan So

Mr. Derick Tse

Ms. Ruth Yee

Mr. Clement Yeung

Henan Provincial Museum

Hong Kong Museum of Art, Urban Council

Hong Kong Tourist Association

Oxford University Press

Public Records Office of Hong Kong

Sam Tung Uk Museum, Regional Council

Tung Chung Primary School

Ms. Chung Lo Mui

Ms. Teresa Coleman

Mrs. Clare Cross

Mr. Niels Cross

Mr. Fung Sau Yan

Mr. Richard J. Garrett

Dr. James W. Hayes

Ms. Lei Lau Mui

Mr. Tim Milnes

Ms. Ng Man Fung

Ms. Tsui Ma Tai

Ms. Tsui Suk Wah

Ms. So Kam Mui

Ms. Wan Yok Lien

Ms. Yuen Suk Ying